MW00778641

Mega Event Planning

Series Editor
Eva Kassens-Noor
Michigan State University
East Lansing, MI, USA

The Mega Event Planning Pivot series will provide a global and cross-disciplinary view into the planning for the world's largest sporting, religious, cultural, and other transformative mega events. Examples include the Olympic Games, Soccer World Cups, Rugby championships, the Commonwealth Games, the Hajj, the World Youth Day, World Expositions, and parades. This series will critically discuss, analyze, and challenge the planning for these events in light of their legacies including the built environment, political structures, socio-economic systems, societal values, personal attitudes, and cultures.

More information about this series at
http://www.palgrave.com/gp/series/14808

James Stout

The Popular Front and the Barcelona 1936 Popular Olympics

Playing as if the World Was Watching

palgrave
macmillan

James Stout
San Diego Mesa College
San Diego, CA, USA

Mega Event Planning
ISBN 978-981-13-8070-9   ISBN 978-981-13-8071-6   (eBook)
https://doi.org/10.1007/978-981-13-8071-6

Cover illustration: © nemesis2207/Fotolia.co.uk

This Palgrave Pivot imprint is published by the registered company Springer Nature
Singapore Pte Ltd.
The registered company address is: 152 Beach Road, #21-01/04 Gateway East, Singapore
189721, Singapore

The original version of the book front matter was revised: The cover credit line has been added. The Correction to the book front matter is available at https://doi.org/10.1007/978-981-13-8071-6_8

To my wife and pets who have suffered Olympian amounts of my complaining during the drafting process.
And
To every young person who has played to win something more than a game.

Preface/Introduction

The Olympics have always been a source of fascination to me. I was five years old when I spent two weeks of my summer watching the world's greatest athletes run, jump, swim, and play in a city that would become my home. Back in 1992, the lasting impact of the Barcelona games on me seemed to be little more than a catchy jingle with which I frustrated my parents and a short-lived attempt at javelin throwing with which I certainly frustrated them when I put an end to my decathlon ambitions and our front window one afternoon. However, what I really got out of those games was one of the earliest experiences of transnationalism that I can conceive of, those BBC montages of little children in Africa, Asia, and the Americas running home to watch the same thing I was watching must have made a profound impact on me, because 25 years later, I still find myself drawn to watch anything, from curling to archery, especially when I have a book I should be writing.

The idea for this book began when, as a young graduate student-athlete, I would spend hours in the archive in Barcelona attempting to studiously chronicle the internal politics of anarchist builders, but often paying more attention to the sports pages at the end of the rolls of microfilm which contained my sources. I was, of course, aware of the Berlin Olympics of 1936, but my readings on the Spanish Second Republic had made nothing more than a cursory mention of the Popular Olympics. As I moved through the microfilms in chronological order, I got closer and closer to the start date of the proposed games until it dawned on me that July 19, 1936, was a date I was familiar with for other reasons. The day that should have been filled with the spirit of fraternity at the opening ceremony instead hosted open hostility as Spain's military turned on its government. I found frustratingly little about the games printed in the days after they were due to begin; understandably, newspapers were consumed with news of the outbreak of war in Spain and the defeat of the coup in Barcelona. I put the study of the games to one side, consigning them to the final chapter of my dissertation as a vision of what might have been. However, as I grew more interested in inter-nationalism and watched the Olympics transform London in 2012 as they had Barcelona in 1992, I kept thinking about what could have been in 1936. Ultimately, the story of the Popular Olympics is as frustrating as it is sad and poetic, but at least it's a story that I have been able to piece together for my own satisfaction, and hopefully that of an English-Language audience.

The world is beginning to see both Catalonia and anti-fascism as it did in the 1930s. Catalonia is, once again, pushing in a different direction from political forces on the right at home and abroad. Once again, the Spanish state is responding to ballots with bullets and batons, and the world is, once again, shrugging its shoulders and looking away. Likewise, anti-fascism, often portrayed as a violent and hateful ideology in the modern media, is once again bringing diverse groups of people into the streets to combat the rhetorical and physical violence that an ideology which created the modern genocide would do to people 70 years after it was defeated in the Second World War. The volunteers who fought for Spain's democracy in the 1930s were labelled "premature antifascists," and it was not until much later that their contribution to global democracy was recognized with the monuments and medals it deserved. The world may not be headed for another conflict, but there is much to be learnt from the way sport and the Olympics were used by those wishing to prevent the last one.

Olympiads are today judged on their legacies. These legacies are measured in quantifiable metrics—sports participation, tourist revenue, usage of venues, and medal counts. However, sometimes the true benefits of a games are intangible. Never has this been truer than in the case of Barcelona 1936. The games never occurred; instead, on the very day that they were due to begin, Spain was plunged into a bloody civil war. However, a games that did not occur can still have a legacy. The Popular Olympics focused the eyes of the progressive world on Barcelona; they filled the city with allies and journalists on the day that it most needed support and someone to share its story. The planning of these games highlights the value that Catalonia placed on sport—the ability of the Olympics to move people from around the world and the potential that such land-mark events have to set a tone for inter-national relations.

This text represents my efforts to understand what the Popular Olympics tell us about the Popular Front, and the ability of playing together to unite people behind a common cause. Beyond the insights that the text will give into the Catalan regime of the Second Republic, it will also offer a perspective on inter-nationalism, anti-fascism, and the potential of mega-events such as Olympiads to serve as tools in the hands of governments and civil society.

San Diego, CA   James Stout

ACKNOWLEDGEMENTS

I feel deeply indebted to so many of my mentors and friends who have helped me along the road to writing this book, in particular to Bernat Lopez Lopez who gave me a place to stay, a great deal of encouragement, a cycling partner, and a much-needed friend at a time when I might otherwise have abandoned this project and many of my other passions. Likewise, to Xavier Pujadas Martí who pointed me towards an area of research which I hope to spend many more years pursuing—sources which have proved invaluable—and most importantly who sat for hours and helped me improve both my research and my Catalan speaking. The financial support of the Anglo-Spanish Society, the HISPANEX grant from the *Ministerio de Educación, Cultura y Deporte* in Spain and the Olympic Studies Center in Lausanne have also been pivotal in making this research, and its continuation, possible. Without the generous support these institutions have provided it would not have been possible to spend the required time in the archive to give a thorough account of an event which only exists in plans and press clippings.

Without the mentorship and support of Robert Edleman I would never have considered sports history a worthy topic. I am forever grateful for the graduate seminar which led to both my dissertation and this text as well as the many spirited dinners and conversations we have enjoyed since then.

Finally, the support of Pamela Radcliff I would never have made it through the marathon of editing, re–editing, and defending my dissertation, nor would my ideas on sport and nationalism be expressed with any degree of clarity or precision. Her willingness to help me express, edit, and have faith in my conclusions deserves mention here.

Contents

ABBREVIATIONS

AAU   Amateur Athletic Union

AEFC   *Acadèmia d'Educació Física de Catalunya* (Physical Education Academy of Catalonia)

AOC   American Olympic Committee

CADCI   *Centre Autonomista de Dependents del Comerç i de la Indústria* (Autonomist Center of Dependents of Commerce and Industry)

CCEP   *Comitè Català pro Esport Popular* (Catalan Committee for Popular Sport)

CEDA   *Confederación Española de Derechas Autónomas* (Spanish Confederation of Autonomous Rights)

CFE   *Club Femeni I d'Esports* (Women's and Sports Club)

CIREO   The *Comité International pour le Respect de l'Espirit Olympique* (International Committee for the Respect of the Olympic Spirit)

CNB   *Club Natació Barcelona* (Barcelona Swimming Club)

CNT   *Confederación Nacional del Trabajo* (National Confederation of Labour)

COC   *Comité Olímpic Català* (Catalan Olympic Committee)

COOP   *Comitè Organitzador de l'Olimpíada Popular* (Committee for the Popular Olympic Games)

DAS   *Gruppe Deutsche Anarcho-Syndikalisten im Ausland* (Group of German Anarchosyndicalists in Exile)

ERC   *Esquerra Republicana de Catalunya* (Catalan Republican Left)

FAI   *Federación Anarquista Ibérica* (Anarchist Federation of Iberia)

FC   Football Club

FCDO   *Federación Cultural Deportiva Obrera* (Spanish Workers' Sport and Cultural Association)

FSGT	*Fédération Sportive et Gymnique du Travail* (Workers' Sporting and Gymnastic Federation)
IOC	International Olympic Committee
NAACP	National Association for the Advancement of Colored People
POUM	*Partido Obrero de Unificatión Marxista* (Workers' Party of Marxist Unification)
RCD	*Real Club Deportivo* (Royal Sports Club)
RSI	Red Sports International
SATUS	*Schweizerischer Arbeiter-, Turn- und Sportverband* (Swiss Workers' Sports Federation)
SWSI	Socialist Workers' Sport International
TUC	Trades Union Congress
YASK	*Yiddiseher Arbeter Sport Klub*

About the Author

James Stout obtained his BA in modern history and politics from Oxford University before writing his PhD at the University of California San Diego. He briefly made a living as an athlete in between his studies and retains a great interest in sport and the identities it can both create and display.

LIST OF FIGURES

CHAPTER 1

Spain and Sport in the 1930s

Abstract The Popular Olympics are often characterized as a part of the Workers' Sport Movement; however, this overlooks the unique circumstances that created a united Popular Front which supported and would have attended these games. This chapter outlines the Spanish and Catalan political situations as well as approaches to sport and nationalism which made it possible to host a global mega-event with less than three months to prepare. Concepts of popular sport, the Popular Front, and Catalan nationalism are explained, and a brief narrative of the history of the Spanish Second Republic will acquaint the reader with the various parties and crises leading up to July 1936.

Keywords Olympics • Catalonia • Popular Front • Popular sport • Spain

Barcelona in 1936 was a city alive with tension. Take a wrong turn off the Ramblas and you might find yourself in any one of a dozen different utopias in the making, or merely relieved of your wallet. The Catalan capital was enjoying a period of relative alignment with Madrid, but this did not mean that civil unrest was uncommon. Police, anarchists, and the military all carried arms and had no qualms about using them against each other or anyone else who crossed their path to a vision of a new Spain or Catalonia. Unions and parties could mobilize huge numbers of people and frequently

© The Author(s) 2020
J. Stout, *The Popular Front and the Barcelona 1936 Popular Olympics*, Mega Event Planning,
https://doi.org/10.1007/978-981-13-8071-6_1

for rallies, protests, and strikes. They did this so often that it was said that Barcelona's paving stones were never fully affixed to the ground as they were merely covering the streets while they waited to be repurposed into another set of barricades.

Those paving stones would be pulled up on the night of July 19, 1936, and they would remain as barricades for the next three years as Barcelona became a battleground between democracy, utopia, and dictatorship in Spain's brutal Civil War (1936–1939). The world engaged with this war too little and too late to stop the coup. Democracies quickly hid behind non-intervention, and the fascist powers quickly mobilized their troops and military hardware. But, for a group of dedicated young people in Barcelona's city park of Montjuïc, none of this would come as a surprise. The anti-fascists, socialists, communists, Jews, people of colour, and political exiles who were gathered in the Hotel Olympic had watched as the world failed to stand up to fascism in the lead up to the Berlin games, and they decided to take a stand. They were in Barcelona to reclaim the spirit of solidarity and brotherhood for the Olympics, and when the time came for rifles to replace running shoes, many of them stood in solidarity there as well. From the very first moments of Spain's conflict, there were international volunteers standing alongside the defenders of the Republic and its flawed but hopeful brand of democracy.

The streets may have been a contested space in the 1930s, but Catalonia's stadia were not. Throughout Spain's Second Republic (1931–1939), Catalonia maintained a left-Republican government under the *Esquerra Republicana de Catalunya* (ERC) that used social policy, charismatic leadership, and physical culture to unite the working and middle classes behind its idea of a nation. From the hard left to the Catholic right, Catalans came to know each other through physical culture. Although this project would never reach its full potential due to the conflict, the short period of its existence saw Catalonia reap the rewards of popular sport and begin its attempts to share this sporting fraternity with other anti-fascist nations around the world.

A major element of the platform of the ERC was popular sport, a form of cross-class physical culture that removed the de facto barriers to entry which existed in sport at the time. Bourgeois sport prized amateurism, civility, and exclusivity. Its adherents dressed fashionably and voted for parties on the right. The Workers' Sport Movement aimed to use sport to teach the working-class solidarity and promote health and strength in working-class youth. Its adherents dressed in overalls and saw barricades, not ballot boxes, as the key to their political liberation. By 1935, the Workers' Sport Movement as a whole contained 4 million members, but nearly half of those were members of clubs in Germany that were prohibited by the Nazis.[1] Bourgeois or elite sport was expensive, and the cost of equipment, membership, and transport often made it inaccessible to the working classes. Workers' Sport was explicitly political and open to only those who shared its Marxist ideology.

As Pujadas and Santacana[2] have shown, Catalan sport grew up outside of an allegiance to inter-national governing bodies or political movements. Sport in Catalonia grew in the inter-war period and lagged behind its neighbours to the north. This meant that inter-national competition was eschewed; instead, Catalan sport was played in and between existing cultural associations, educational institutions, workplaces, professional organizations, unions, labour exchanges, and neighbourhood groups. This sporting practice united classes and ideologies on the playing fields and played a role in the growing sense of cross-class national identity that grew before and during the Republic. With the arrival of the Republic and the installation of a progressive left-Republican government in Barcelona, this sporting practice gained a name, an organizational structure, and an ideology; popular sport aimed to bring together bourgeois and working-class athletes, promote public health, and foster a sense of shared identity that saw a national and progressive identity overcome class and political divisions.

To paraphrase Rogers Brubaker,[3] identity is not a thing in the world but a perspective on the world. The perspective on the world that the ERC created was one of optimism for a future when Catalonia and Spain, and the other nations of the world, could coexist in democratic fraternity. It is the creation of this perspective that I shall seek to explain in this chapter. Governments across the world engaged in the process of "nationalizing" the masses in the early twentieth century. The use of competitive sport and non-competitive physical culture to serve the end of nationalizing the masses and to forge a cross-class shared identity was by no means unique to Catalonia, or the Second Republic, but it did meet with great success there. In the years between Primo de Rivera's military dictatorship (1923–1930) and Spain's descent into war in 1936, the national ambitions of the Catalans were founded on and exhibited in the sporting world as much as the political one. This chapter will investigate how this Catalan sporting nation developed, and how Catalonia planned to share that sporting solidarity with the rest of the world through the Popular Olympics.

THE SECOND REPUBLIC

In the spring air of 1931, Spain's town halls were filled with the new Republican tricolours and its citizens filled with a sense of hope for the future. Following municipal elections in April, King Alfonso XIII had fled the country. Just a year before, the monarch and the military had withdrawn their support from the dictatorship of General Primo de Rivera. With the removal of political authority, Spain had to decide how it wished to engage with itself and the world. Very quickly it became clear that beneath the Republic's flag were two Spains with mutually incompatible ideas. Catalonia's politics was very much tied to the left-Republican conception of a Spain that embraced the secular Republic and the ideals of liberty, equality, and fraternity that it had inherited from its predecessors. The other Spain strongly opposed Catalan autonomy, agnostic politics, and the socially progressive agenda that united much of the centre and left. In many cases, the so-called accidentalist right also saw the Republic itself as a means, not an end. This conflict about what Spanishness meant was to characterize and destroy the Republic.

Our opinions of the Second Republic have changed as we have changed the perspective from which we view it. In the Franco era, it was constructed as a chaotic time of left-wing maximalism that placed revolutionary ideology above the rights of the people and the day-to-day running of the country. In Spain's post-dictatorship, the Republic has come to be seen as a more well-intentioned experiment in social democracy, albeit one that lacked the support of large sectors of society.

The Republic and its governments can be split into three two-year periods, generally known as the First (or reformist), Second (or "black"), and Third Biennia (the Third Biennium is also known as the Popular Front government). Each one of these periods was defined by a change in government and ideology and a vastly different idea about Spain's future.

Hours before the Second Republic was proclaimed in Madrid, Catalan hero and president-to-be Francesc Macià proclaimed the Catalan Republic, within a confederation with the other peoples of Spain. Although Macià's confederation would not last long, Catalonia gained much autonomy under the Republican constitution that was later approved and was able to work on the left-Republican goals of education, land reform, an agnostic state, and improvements in the "condition of the people" for five years before Spain's military rose against its government.

Catalonia's regional government, the *Generalitat*, and Spain's national government, the *Cortes*, were elected on different cycles with elections at least once per year for the first three years of the Republic (June 1931, November 1932, and November 1933). This resulted in instability and a constantly changing relationship. Catalonia remained stable, thanks to the "big tent" of the ERC which united a broad range of groups on the left of the Republic. Long before the Spanish left came together in the Popular Front of 1936, the ERC formed a catch-all alliance that proved insurmountable in the Generalitat, gaining the most Catalan votes in all three Catalan elections. There was a considerable fluctuation in votes for the more conservative Catalanist party the *Lliga Regionalista de Catalunya*. Indeed, the Lliga gained one more seat than the ERC in the 1933 Spanish general election. However, the Lliga could not repeat this result in the Generalitat, where the ERC held a tight grip throughout the Republic.

In Madrid, politics showed a lot less unity. The 1931 election was swept by groups on the left of the Republic in both Spain and Catalonia and gave rise to a liberal constitution which upheld the rights of the citizen and reduced the special rights that the Catholic Church had come to expect. The first government was formed of a Liberal-Socialist coalition that focused on a social democratic, reformist, and an anti-clerical agenda. Education was a key goal and an important tool of this government; they aimed to remove the religious bent of instruction and to offer a Republican education that would "consolidate a class divided nation."[4]

The church had been so closely tied to Spanishness that it was "not so much a religion as a culture"[5]; for some on the religious right, the church and the nation were inseparable. For legislators who held this belief, the policies of the First Biennium were not just disagreeable, they were sacrilegious. Sadly, national consolidation and many of the other goals of the first government did not come as rapidly as promised. Landowners and the church felt alienated by rapid change, whilst the working classes were often angered by the slow pace of promised reforms. Both those opposed to and supporting the regime seemed happy to place results ahead of rules in their attempt to assert their own vision of the Spain they wanted. On the left, there was working-class protest and clamour for a more equitable distribution of land and profits; this met with a swift and often violent government response. The authoritarian policing techniques favoured by the new regime led to it being dubbed the "Republic of order" and alienating many of the working classes who preferred to take their chances at the barricades than vote for a different set of people to mete out the same violence and poverty they had known for generations.

The year 1933 saw voters elect a government that had a dramatically different vision of Spain. Many on the left called for workers to boycott the vote altogether. One newspaper proclaimed "Parliament... is a filthy house of prostitution."[6] Dissatisfaction with the pace of reform on the left and anger at the previous administration on the right heralded the beginning of the Republic's Second Biennium and saw the Catholic conservative *Confederación Española de Derechas Autónomas* (CEDA), which looked to Carlism and fascism for inspiration, return as the biggest party. CEDA's partial commitment to the Republic caused President Zamora to refuse to appoint their leader as prime minister. Instead, Zamora selected veteran Radical Republican populist and dedicated anti-Catalanist Alejandro Lerroux with a promise of a "republic for all Spaniards"[7] that immediately rung hollow as it divided the nation and party. During this two-year period, known as the "*bienio negro*," the Socialists moved from protest to insurrection and Spain began to splinter into a series of groups who considered their political opposition and the Republic to be expendable in the pursuit of their goals.

This spirit of insurrection took hold in Catalonia. Following the death of Macià in 1933, Lluís Companys took the reins of the ERC, and it moved even further away from the old Catalanism of the Lliga and closer to the social democratic ideology that helped his party gain support among the working classes. A squabble with the CEDA government in Madrid over the rights of certain tenant farmers became a conflict that, on October 6, spilled from the pages of newspapers to the streets of Barcelona as Companys declared the Catalan state within a Spanish Federal Republic. The Catalan police force, local youth groups, and union militias took to the streets. In theory, there were 70,000 loyal workers at the disposal of the ERC, but the better armed and organized anarchists remained aloof.[8] This left-wing factionalism, which would plague much of Europe for decades, would cost the people of Catalonia their independence. Within an hour of the proclamation, martial law was declared and light artillery was directed at the Generalitat. The idea of a Catalan state died at the barricades in short order. By **6 a.m.**, Companys had surrendered, and would later be sentenced to 30 years in prison. By December, all autonomous powers given to Catalonia were revoked and returned to Madrid. From then until the 1936 elections, Madrid would appoint a governor-general of Catalonia.

Two days before the rising in Catalonia, a worker's militia led by miners took up arms against the government in Asturias. The socialists in Asturias were joined by the local anarchists and successfully set up soviets to run the cities they held. Their columns marched into Oviedo on October 6 and overwhelmed the government garrison. Franco himself led Moroccan troops in what he called a "frontier war"[9] against the miners and subdued them only with considerable loss of life on both sides. It is telling that Franco used the regular troops from Morocco and not the peninsular army, as the latter was thought to be at a tactical disadvantage facing the miners with their skilled use of dynamite. Ultimately, the miners were defeated, with up to 4000 killed and ten times as many sent to prison. However, the Asturian miners became a touchstone for the power of the people in arms. Clearly, both of the "two Spains" had decided that the rules of the game were less important than the outcome. In response to the failed insurrections of the left, there was a growth in the catastrophist right and a move away from peaceful dialogue. This, combined with a gambling scandal that removed the Radical party from power, caused the dissolution of the government and a fresh round of elections in a hugely divided Spain. What was at stake was not just the composition of the government, but the future of the nation.

The 1936 vote returned Spain's Popular Front government. Despite a composition very similar to the government of the First Biennium (albeit without the radicals and with the communists), policy was now focused on opposition to fascism and not a desire for a new Spain. Under this government, language of class conflict was played down in favour of talk of rights and democracy. Even the anarcho-syndicalist *Confederación Nacional del Trabajo* (CNT), long-time proponents of more radical reform than liberal politics offered, soft-pedalled their abstention campaigns in favour of voting "against fascism."[10] This government showed that the working classes' best interests lay with support of the institutions. Companys and 30,000 more prisoners were released, public works and education projects were resumed, and land reform was accelerated. Catalonia regained its right to autonomous government, and the work of social reform and addressing the injustices of the previous two years began.

This government's biennium would be both longer and shorter than intended; just 5 months after it was elected, the government would rely on the same left-wing alliance that secured it victory at the ballot box to defend that victory at the barricades. In Madrid, a lieutenant of the Assault Guards was shot by a Falangist; in recrimination a monarchist member of

Parliament, José Calvo Sotelo, was executed by the Assault Guards. This spark landed on the dry leaves of rightist, religious, and royalist sentiment in the military, and a long-planned coup was launched. First in Morocco and then in the mainland the military turned against its government. The government at first wavered and then armed the people; these people were able to suppress the rising in all the major industrial areas and cities with the exception of Seville. German aircraft allowed the much more professional and experienced Army of Africa to participate in the first major military airborne operation and secure much of the north and west of Spain. With the nation now divided in the ideological and physical sense, the stage was set for a conflict between democracy and dictatorship that had much in common with the later global conflict over the same issues.

In Barcelona, the armed unions and loyal police and air forces of the Republic retained control of the city. The military deployment had been chaotic, and the anarchists prepared. As troops marched towards the Plaça de Catalunya, they were attacked with homemade grenades. Bloody struggles over the telephone exchange and hotels in the city centre followed. General Goded, who had arrived earlier that day to lead the rebels, surrendered when all the rebel-held buildings were surrounded by police and anarchists. Goded broadcast a message on the radio telling his troops to stand down, and the anarchist militias wiped up the last of the rebels at their barracks the next day. The leaders of the coup who had been captured in Catalonia were imprisoned in Montjuïc, and then on the prison ship *Uruguay* (where they gave fascist salutes to passing Italian ships) before being tried in court and executed in the moat of the Montjuïc castle.[11]

These arrests and executions did not put an end to the conflict in Spain; rather, they were just the beginning of three long years of bloodshed in which both sides would attempt to court the support of the inter-national forces who were squaring off in anticipation of the war which was soon to engulf Europe. The Republic would rely on Mexico, the Soviet Union, and foreign volunteers. In contrast, the rebels would enjoy the support of Italy, Germany, and Portugal as well as the complicity that came from British and French non-intervention. There would be mass killings, mass graves, and the innovation of many of the means of mass murder which would come to characterize the Second World War. Barcelona would remain in the hands of the Republic until January 1939. From the fall of Catalonia's capital until the death of Franco, and in many ways long after his departure, the city and nation would remain suppressed and without the autonomy that they fought for on the opening day of the Popular Olympics.

Catalan Nationalism in the Second Republic

To understand the changes in the Catalan nation over this period, we must grasp the concept of nationalism. Nations are nothing more than narratives, stories we tell ourselves about who we are. To be more specific, a nation, as I shall use the term here, is the idea of shared community, heritage, and identity that links people across time and space and binds them in a common future. A nation will sometimes, but not always, be linked to a nation-based political movement, a nationalism. Nationalism need not struggle for a nation state. Nationalism may seek functional autonomy in certain spheres, often those of language, education, and culture, but need not aim for a complete state apparatus.

Given the results of the Civil War, it is easy to look back on the Second Republic as doomed from the outset. But in order to understand the crowds who welcomed the Republic in 1931, we have to understand the hope for the future that engulfed a nation emerging from a military dictatorship. Just days before the first elections of the Republic, Macià had formed a party that combined the majority of bourgeois nationalists with the elements of the left that were committed to the new system. His party, the ERC, fused his *Estat Català* with the *Partit Republicà Català* of his soon-to-be successor Lluís Companys and the more diverse regional group associated with the publication *L'Opinió*. While the rest of Spain was subdividing into an alphabet soup of different ideologies and parties, the big tent of the ERC's nationalist-left-Republican ideology managed to consistently unite Catalonia's voters, and it remained in power for the duration of the Republic.

Unity was by no means absolute, and major opposition came from the left. The Catalan working classes and many of their unions were not as influenced by the Soviet communism as their European counterparts. Instead, many subscribed to the anarcho-syndicalist model. Conflicts within the left were common and hinged on the degree to which groups were prepared to commit to revolution or accept the Republic and negotiate with employers. More radical elements of the loosely federated *Federación Anarquista Ibérica* (FAI) remained aloof from negotiations and dedicated to the "revolutionary gymnastics" and "propaganda of the deed" that saw them express themselves through bullets and not ballots. Meanwhile, the CNT showed a greater willingness to negotiate but still often bolstered its position with strikes and refusal to cooperate with the government. Both groups found themselves frequently in conflict with employers, police, and each other.

In the decades before the Second Republic, Catalan nationalism, much like Catalan politics, was divided along class lines. Although Catalonia had a history of distinct rights and assertion of a separateness from Spain, Catalan nationalism really began its modern resurgence when Spain faced its *Annus Mirablis* in 1898. With Spain facing economic and imperial downfall, Catalonia's "precocious capitalism"[12] and industrial prowess stood in sharp contrast. Out of this disparity emerged the *Lliga Regionalista*, a political party which wanted Catalan elites to lead, not leave, Spain. The resurgence in Catalan nationalism may have come from an economic crisis, and at first taken the form of an elite political pressure group, but it had roots in a cultural bloom known as the *Renaixença* or Renaissance. This romantic revivalist movement recovered the medieval idea of *Jocs Florals* (floral games), a kind of poetic contest with the theme of *Patria, Fides, Amor* (Country, Faith, Love). At the same time, academics began focusing on restoring the Catalan language, and there was a resurgence in Catalan choral societies and traditional dances that gave a cultural backbone to Catalonia's distinct economic identity. This invention of tradition began as nothing more than an assertion of Catalan character with no intent of asserting political independence, but cultural unity among the middle and upper classes provided an important groundwork for what would become an independent and assertive Catalan identity. By the early decades of the twentieth century, Catalonia was not a state trying to create a nation so much as a distinct cultural and economic elite trying to phrase its concerns in national terms. Like many other entrepreneurs of identity, these elites relied upon culture as much as politics to advance their idea of Catalan belonging.

Catalonia had long been at the forefront of Spain's industrial economy, and, by the 1930s, this meant that a considerable proportion of its working class was made up of migrants from elsewhere in Spain. Catalan nationalism changed in its encounter with democratic politics and demographic growth. Under the ERC, the Catalan nation was constructed as cross-class, popular, and committed to democracy. This politics saw Catalonia as a distinct nation from Spain, but one that could coexist with a Spanish state that shared its goals and did not impede its social progress. In the Republic, Catalan nationalism pursued its goal of nation-building within the Spanish state when the government in Madrid acquiesced and asserted a more independent identity when faced with chauvinistic nationalism in Madrid. In 1934, Catalonia asserted its independence from Madrid at the barricades; by 1936, Barcelona and Madrid would come together to promote the idea of fraternal nationalism under the umbrella of a broad ideological consensus and a passionate opposition to fascism.

Catalan nationalism has always been something of a concept of "calculated vagueness,"[13] but it was in this period that the nation attained its most solid form. Building a nation without the entire apparatus of state left the ERC with a challenge. Weber highlights the importance of tools such as the military, transport networks, and schools in his excellent study of the nationalization of the French peasantry.[14] These tools were not available in Catalonia, and the Catalan language was by no means universal among the working class, making the use of print capitalism alone less feasible.[15] In their place, the ERC turned to culture, particularly physical culture, to build a nation. Just as poetry and singing and the associated invention of tradition had helped elites to gel, the ERC hoped that sport and physical culture would bring the masses into their big tent. Culture comes as much from below as from above, and it is through this cultural construction of Catalan identity that a discourse emerged between high and low culture, between bourgeois and proletariat, and between factory worker and politician. In this discourse, Catalan identity was co-created and born as a cross-class and welcoming nationalism based on shared values, not shared bloodlines. It was this cross-class nation, with its roots in playing fields and gymnasia, that stood up to Hitler's ethnic and exclusive ideas of the nation.

THE OLYMPIC MOVEMENT

Today, we take the close relationship between sport and nationalism for granted. The inclusion of flags at the Olympics and national anthems at games, and fans in the stands cheering their country people on seem natural. Both sport and political nationalism emerged at roughly the same time, and they grew up supporting each other in the uncertain early period of industrial modernity. As the economy moved from the less rigid discipline of proto industry to the regulated environment of the factory, so activity moved from the exuberance of play to bounded discipline and competition of sport. Sport largely won out over less competitive forms of physical culture such as the German *Turnen* movement, and in many ways, the competitive and standardized world of sport paralleled the growth of capitalism. Rules about who could play and how they could win developed alongside rules about who could be part of and in charge of nations. Theories have long linked the nation to modernity,[16] and specific elements of modernity such as the press, but the nationalizing potential of sports has often been overlooked. On the pitches and terraces, the abstract idea of a nation can take physical form and be experienced. This nation can be consolidated through the media as it comes together in support of its heroes. War may have forged nations, but Orwell aptly called sport "war minus the shooting,"[17] and certainly both served important national and inter-national functions by 1936.

Hobsbawm, in his work on the invention of traditions, has shown the value of invented traditions and a mythical past in creating a sense of national unity in the present and the particular fervour for the invention of a mythical past in the early industrial years of the last century.[18] Sport plays an important role in creating modern nations as it gives us heroes, myths, and practices to share. Cronin[19] has illustrated that, much like primordial nationalists, entrepreneurs of sporting national identity will claim links to a mythical past in order to bolster their hold on identity in the present. In both cases sport has bridged a gap between political and cultural nationalism and helped make nationalism a mass phenomenon in the age of democracy. James[20] and Thompson,[21] among others, have shown the value of sport in creating a nation in the modern era. National sports, and inter-national competition, both help to create a simultaneous national experience, embed national values, and define common heroes and enemies.

The modern Olympics are very much creatures of the growth of capitalism, nationalism, and the networks that connect the two. Baron Pierre de Coubertin founded the International Olympic Committee (IOC) in 1894, and the first of the modern games were held in Athens in 1896. These events drew on French Republican Olympiads, British festival games (including the Much Wenlock Olympic Games), and the Greek interest in a classical revival which had existed since their independence from the Ottoman Empire. De Coubertin's games began as a mixture of pseudo-Hellenic paganism, the worship of European masculinity, and a gathering place for the transnational bourgeoisie. De Coubertin himself, a curious product of a Jesuit education and studies at Paris' École Libre, was engaged in a search for a new Olympia in the religious as well as the sporting sense, and in his games he created new deities and a new mountain on which to elevate them.

The first modern Olympic Games in 1896 were funded by wealthy philanthropists and the Greek government but were far from the spectacle they are today. Their rhetoric was of inter-national peace, celebrating the human spirit and creating a contest that rewarded excellence and eschewed the impure influences of money and power. In reality, the games did bring together a huge crowd, but they excluded women and most countries outside of the core capitalist states. The subsequent two Olympiads, in Paris and St Louis, were merely side shows to the Expositions those two cities held and took place over months, providing amusing side shows to the commercial gatherings rather than a concentrated cultural festival. The games, and their organizing committee, reflected the spirit of their era, one of imperialist capitalism and equality amongst all people who were considered human, which is to say the upper- and middle-class men of Europe and the Americas. The 1904 St. Louis games included an exhibition of Indigenous peoples competing against people of European descent in events that they had never before practised.[22]

The IOC reflected the initial impetus behind much of modern sport, which was the "Muscular Christianity" championed by Thomas Arnold and the British boarding school system and fuelled by the European elites who worried that their nations' populace and potential soldiery were becoming enfeebled by the lifestyle changes associated with industrialization. Both of these impulses were deeply rooted in the European desire to continue churning about a great number of gentlemen of distinction to run their growing empires and to "civilizing" local elites into the sort of people who obeyed rules, respected authority, and applauded a good cover drive. To this end, the games, even as sport became more accessible to the working classes in the early twentieth century, retained a strict policy of allowing only amateur athletes. Amateurism was a code for making sure sport remained the domain of those with the time and resources to practise sport merely as a leisure activity.[23] This commitment to keeping the games an elite concern didn't seem to stop the governing bodies involved from demonstrating an equally deep commitment to talking about public health and the well-being of the working classes.

The games resembled a gentlemen's club in more than their class make up. Although the first Olympic Games were an all-male affair, these sporting gentlemen were joined by ladies in some events thereafter. However, by 1932, fewer than 10% of Olympians were women, and the events that these pioneering women could compete numbered only 14, as opposed to the 103 that were open to men.[24] Where male athletes could expect positive reflections on their bodies and character almost regardless of the result, women were far more likely to receive a public dressing-down as they neglected their domestic responsibilities to undertake distinctly unladylike contests at the games. Even as women entered the workforce and the political realm, the IOC dug in its heels and staunchly defended its pseudo-scientific sexism. Indeed, it was not until 2012 that women and men could compete for the same number of medals.

The image of the games as something belonging to the world was one that De Coubertin had always tried to cultivate. As Keys[25] has argued, it was not really until the Los Angeles games of 1932 that the games took on a global appeal, thanks to the organization and commercialization of Hollywood which delivered a global Olympic spectacle. However, amateurism rules and the expense of attending the games kept them a largely Caucasian affair, with notable (and much were they noted in the contemporary press) exceptions ranging from Japanese swimmers and runners of African extraction until the post-war era.[26] The success of these much-maligned groups, rather than pushing for equality, led to white masculinity reflecting on how it had lost despite its inherent superiority. In his popular syndicated telegram, Hollywood star Will Rogers quipped "wait 'till we get to golf, bridge or cocktail shaking, then the American white man will come into his own."[27]

However, the games established themselves in the eyes of much of the world as an event that celebrated global unity. With De Coubertin's high-minded rhetoric, he gave the games the image of a festival to celebrate the sporting and human spirit rather than the unleashing of unbridled competition. The baron famously pontificated that "the most important thing in the Olympic Games is not winning but taking part; the essential thing in life is not conquering but fighting well."[28] For the newspaper-consuming transnational bourgeoisie, the games became sacred, and this made them a platform from which nations and athletes could project their moral and spiritual as well as sporting prowess.

The gap between De Coubertin's stated desire that "the Olympic torch pursue its way through ages, increasing friendly understanding among nations, for the good of a humanity always more enthusiastic, more courageous and more pure,"[29] and the unwillingness of the IOC to remove the games from Nazi-controlled Berlin in 1936 highlighted the inconsistencies in Olympic rhetoric and reality. It was this gap that allowed the Popular Olympics to claim that "The Olympic Spirit is in Barcelona, not Berlin."[30]

Sport in Spanish and Catalan Nations

Weber, Anderson, and others have long posited education, print capitalism, the military, and transport networks as important agents of nationalization in the nineteenth and twentieth centuries. Sport in early twentieth-century Spain was, as McFarland has illustrated, a way of communicating modernity and belonging to the growing middle class.[31] As the Catalan nation grew, so did democratic politics. In the absence of a shared national language (most immigrants to Catalonia spoke very little Catalan until the late 1990s), the nation needed to find a way to appeal to the working classes if it was to survive the move from elite to democratic politics. It was in this search for a unifying passion that sport emerged. People might not be seeing the same operas or reading the same books, but they were often playing the same games.

Sport in Iberia in general, and the Popular Olympics in particular, have seen an upsurge in interest in recent years. This book aims to build on the works of Gounot, Pujadas, Santacana, Hargreaves, and others which have established the value of sport in Catalan identity and the importance of the Popular Olympics in the history of both sport, Spain, the Olympics, and the Popular Front.[32]

Before the Republic, there was significant interest in hosting the Olympic Games on the part of the Catalan-identifying elites associated with the Lliga. Later, this was taken up by the *Mancommunitat*, the Catalan parliament of the time, and by aristocrats during the dictatorship of Primo de Rivera. It was civil society that funded these bids and the construction of much of the infrastructure that the popular sport movement would later depend on. Initially, this impulse was essentially a bourgeois innovation that aimed to enhance the inter-national status of Catalonia and cement its links to northern European economies by hosting the celebration of bourgeois leisure and reaffirmation of class status that the IOC's games had become. It was not until the Republic that the hosting of events took on a popular ideology.

The enthusiasm for sport in Barcelona was not always shared by Madrid. Indeed, as the Catalans were building stadia and agitating to host the Olympics, elites in Madrid were arguing about whether it was even worth attending the 1928 Antwerp Games.[33] The government's lack of willingness to support sport and the associated infrastructure did not prevent football from gaining popular and financial support as well as an associated press and powerful following among the working classes by the start of the Second Republic.[34] However, it was not until Catalonia gained significant autonomy that government initiatives included sport.

For as long as there has been a football club in Barcelona and Madrid, they have hated each other. This rivalry has not always been national in character; it is natural for there to be a simple sporting rivalry between the two biggest teams in Spain and their respective fan bases. However, just about every time there has been a dictator in Madrid, this rivalry has become especially fierce, and standing on the terraces has become a political act. Primo de Rivera banned FC Barcelona in 1925 when the Spanish national anthem was met with a chorus of whistles from Catalan fans. The club founder and chairman, Joan Gamper, was driven to suicide by the accusations that followed this incident. In the early months of the civil war, Josep Sunyol became the second chairman of the club to fall victim to the Spanish right; he was executed in August 1936.[35] Even today, FC Barcelona is an icon for the Catalan nation, with the club issuing a firm statement in support of the Catalan independence referendum in 2017.[36]

It was not just in FC Barcelona's stadium, Les Corts, that Catalan nationalism and Catalan sport went hand in hand. In the 1930s, the move from the Lliga's conception of an elite nation to the ERC's goal of substantive democratic Catalan national identity allowed for, and was aided by, the expansion of a national sporting identity. As Bunk illustrates, intellectual and cultural elites had remained relatively aloof from mass sports in earlier decades, but in the search for cultural unity, it seems that they began to see value in the passions of the crowds who would fill Les Corts and thousands of less glamorous pitches every weekend.[37] As Catalan daily *La Rambla* gushed in the first hours of the Republic, "there comes a time when sport is the only mouthpiece for a nation which desires liberty and justice... A sporting nation is one which is conscious of both its rights and duties."[38] This caption was followed by a photo of Macià himself, along with the first Prime Minister (and later President) of the Second Republic Niceto Alcalá-Zamora y Torres, and a team of sweaty young men in striped shirts. This wasn't the regimented physical culture of fascism or communism; this was a physical embodiment of the youthful exuberance of the newly empowered nation.

The national self-perception of Catalonia has long been a dichotomy between *seny* (sensibleness or well-considered action) and *rauxa* (umbrage or sudden capricious action). Both of these characteristics were commonly attributed to elite athletes and popular sporting organizations in the Catalan media of the Second Republic.[39] This allowed the creation of national heroes and archetypes to whom the new Catalans could look up and the personification of the national traits to which they could aspire. When newspapers reflected on the efforts of cyclist Mariano Cañardo, his calculating tactics and exuberant attacks were recounted with glee. The hard-working and successful immigrant from Navarre, who self-identified as Catalan and found the Catalan public more than willing to accept him into their nation and their hearts, was the platonic ideal of a Catalan citizen in the ERC's model. When he received awards for his racing from Macià in the early days of the Republic, it was as if old and new Catalanism had come together through the two men. When Cañardo came second in the 1935 cycling Tour of Spain, he elected not to celebrate in Madrid's bars but behind bars instead. Cañardo took his trophy to Lluís Companys as the Catalan leader sat in prison following his role in the events of October 1934.[40] It was through these heroes of popular Catalan identity in sport as well as politics that the ERC gave body to its model of the ideal Catalan.

Catalonia had not integrated into inter-national sports networks like the French, British, and German sporting organizations had. Elite sporting organizations, including those for rugby[41] and football, didn't accept Catalan teams, and the relatively late development of sport in Iberia meant that many were not that competitive inter-nationally. The relatively minor impact of communism, especially in Catalonia, meant that Workers' Sport was not a string force either. The *Federación Cultural Deportiva Obrera* (Spanish Workers' Sport and Cultural Association/FCDO) counted only 9000 members in 1933, and 5000 of those were in Madrid[42]; indeed, it did not open a Catalan branch until 1934. Instead, Catalan sport grew up among unions, political parties, cultural organizations, and professional groups. Without inter-national competition, these groups played one another without the divisions of class or the strict rules of amateurism. From this cross-class unity grew the popular sports movement and, to an extent, the modern Catalan nation. The closest analogue, and one the Catalans explicitly modelled their sporting practices on, was the model of the Czech Sokol founded by Miroslav Tyrs which had been pivotal in that nation's independence movement.[43] This movement had roots before the republic; however, it gained not only adherents but also institutional representation, political purpose, and a more explicit leadership and ideology under the ERC.

Citius, Altius, Fortius was the motto of the Olympic movement at its inception; later, language was added about taking part as well as winning when Coubertin was inspired by the Bishop of Pennsylvania's speech at the London 1908 games.[44] In Catalonia, the process was reversed, and sport focused on fairness and inclusivity first and found performance little more than a pleasant side effect of participation. The ERC's sporting identity encompassed both mass participation popular sport and elite sports where the masses were confined to the role of spectators. Elite sport would give examples of hard-working and successful Catalan idols. Popular sport aimed to create a happier, healthier, and more Catalan-identifying citizenry and to build stronger cross-class communities rather than champion athletes. Goals were set in terms of participation, engagement of women, reduction of illness and disease, and formation of young citizens rather than distances, points, or times. Citizens of all levels, ages, and genders would come to better know and understand each other through shared gymnastics, swimming lessons, and running races. This was the kinder, gentler face of the Republic, and it aimed to obtain consent of the working class for the new state rather than coerce the masses into obedience.

Popular sports organizations fell into five major categories: single sport clubs, multipurpose voluntary associations that included sport or physical culture, trade union–based centres, popular sections of elite sports clubs, and sports federations or governing bodies. Each of these served to not only enhance and broaden sports participation but serve as a classroom for democracy. Members of clubs or organizations would debate, vote, and engage in democratic practices in the club, and learn fraternity and civility through these civil society institutions.

At the heart of popular sport was a focus on improvement of the citizenry through physical culture. The emphasis was not on the record performance so much as the collective experience. Sports such as gymnastics, swimming, running, tug of war, and football were popular and affordable. They were seen to balance the asymmetries and ailments caused by industrial labour. Popular sport celebrated the popular athlete, who was a member of the nation and probably a union as well as a team and who measured success in progress, not performances. Popular sporting organizations aimed to bring classes together and foster a climate of mutual understanding through shared experience. Coaching, equipment, and a good dose of political rhetoric were provided to all members at an affordable membership fee.

The popular sport movement was explicit in its opposition to the militarization of sport. The programme of the Popular Olympics stated that

[t]he working masses intend to counteract the harmful effect of their hard toil by sporting activities and now with the exception of a few countries the world recognizes the vital importance of sport to the health and culture of the broad masses. It is shameful that in present day society there are elements who abuse sport, exploiting it for their militaristic and warlike ends. Taking advantage of the eagerness and enthusiasm for sport they lead the

youth along the road to war. Under the pretext of strengthening their bodies and adding happiness to their lives, they systematically subject the youth
[to] a strict military discipline and a thorough technical and ideological
preparation for future wars.[45]

Sport was, in the eyes of those constructing a cross-class sporting nation
in Catalonia, a unifying force, not a divisive one.

The movement also distinguished itself from elite sports at the time
with its full inclusion of women's sport and athletes. Women stood alongside men in the playing fields of Catalonia and on the posters of the 1936
Popular Olympics; later they would stand side by side on the barricades
and in the trenches. Through organizations such as the *Club Femeni I
d'Esports* (Feminist and Sports Club/CFE) as well as progressive legisla-
tion with regard to women's rights and marriage, the ERC established a
goal of progress towards gender equality. Women's sport was given attention in the sporting press, and funding was provided for women's events
whenever a multisport competition was held. Although participation
lagged behind men, there was considerable growth in the relatively short
lifespan of the Republic. It was the women who grew up in Catalonia's
popular sports clubs who took to the barricades in 1936 as the famed
milicianas (women soldiers) of the popular militia.[46]

Many of the stadia and facilities used by the popular sports organizations
(and later the Popular Olympics) were constructed using the finances of
Catalan elites. In 1929 Barcelona hosted an inter-national exposition at
huge expense with the goal of promoting Catalan industry. These expositions were temporary hubs of global industrial capitalism and played a huge
role in globalizing both products and culture and constructing both
metropoles and colonies in the eyes of the citizens of host nations. Many of
the buildings, including the Montjuïc Stadium, that had been built to unite
the transnational bourgeoisie in 1929 would go on to be repurposed for
popular sport and the Popular Olympics. Ironically, it was the Popular
Olympics, with their cross-class intentions and total lack of concern for
profitability, that alloyed Barcelona, Paris, London, and Madrid in the pro-
motion of an event that welcomed the world and not their bourgeois forbears.

POPULAR FRONTISM

As Leon Blum indicated in 1942, "[the Popular Front coalition] was a
reflex of instinctive defense against the dangers which threatened French
Republican institutions, and liberty itself."[47] Much the same could be said

for ERC, which came together to oppose classism and militarism and support a cross-class and substantive democratic ideal. Indeed, the Popular Olympics themselves came together a few weeks before Blum's government and aimed to defend not just the French Republic but democratic ideals across the world. To do so, they would follow the political example established by the Popular Front policy which aimed to minimize left-wing factionalism and replace it with a robust anti-fascist coalition.

The Popular Front policy emerged from the Seventh World Congress of the Communist International 1935. Under the leadership of German communist George Dimtriov, the "The People's Front Against Fascism and War" was proclaimed to prevent a repeat of what had happened in Germany where the left had been swept away by the populism and pageantry of the new threat from the fascist far-right. Communist parties were instructed to ally with socialist and even bourgeois liberal parties in order to secure social progress at home and halt the rise of fascism across Europe. In the depression-struck new democracies of Europe, communists would use this policy to embrace nationalism and step back from anti-capitalist maximalism in favour of a slower but more secure progress and a bulwark against the spread of fascism.[48] On the sports pitches, it meant a withdrawal from separate sporting spheres and an embrace of any sporting institution that favoured competition for all and opposed the games, and ideology, in Berlin.

Leon Blum's French government included socialists, radicals, and communists when it came to power in 1936, but it was far from the only Popular Front that stood for office. In Spain, the Popular Front was also elected in 1936 and united communists, non-Stalinist communists, anarcho-syndicalists, and socialists. The ERC, with its relatively broad church, was part of the coalition in Madrid. In the spirit of anti-fascism, the ERC also began to make common cause with the CNT and anarchists in Barcelona. In the UK, elements of the Labour, Liberal, Communist, and Independent Labour Parties joined with some conservatives, including Winston Churchill, to form a Popular Front against appeasement of fascism. There were also Popular Front movements outside of Europe, with the presidency of Chile held by a Popular Front coalition and the Communist Party of the USA joining forces with the Socialist Party, embracing nationalism, and supporting Roosevelt's New Deal. All around the world, securing progress and opposing the growth of fascism helped the left overcome its factional disagreements in favour of presenting a united front.

The Popular Front was an initiative of the Communist International but by no means a tool of Moscow. It was a recognition on the part of doctrinaire Marxist-Leninism that it must relinquish its strict steering of national parties along the path to utopia if it wished to avoid the fracturing of the left that had allowed the right to seize power in Germany. The Popular Front saw value in alliances with bourgeois liberals and socialists, and it took the sporting unity that the Workers' Olympics had given the working class and shared it with a broader inter-national coalition. In this atmosphere of broad coalition politics and coming together based on what was shared, not what was not, the ERC was well placed to offer a platform for popular physical culture which would give a body to the Popular Front just as it had to the Catalan nation.

1936

By 1936 the Popular Front was up and running, but it had some distance to make up on fascism. Not only had the right taken power in Germany and Italy, but the UK, USA, and their allied democratic powers were tired of war and had made the decision to appease rather than confront the ideology. Fear of communism after the Russian revolution compounded the idea that fascism would serve as a bulwark to revolution that was more amenable to capitalism than the left-wing alternative. In both Spain and France, Popular Front governments were elected despite a significant challenge from fascist or fascist-like movements on the populist right. Oswald Mosley's British Union of Fascists would engage in anti-Semitic rioting in October of that year, and groups such as the German American Bund in the USA supported and styled themselves after fascists in Europe. Liberal democracy was facing its first real crisis, and as this was reaching a peak, one of the early institutions of liberal inter-nationalism, the Olympic Games, had fallen into the hands of the Nazis.

The policy of appeasement of fascists was not universally popular. When a German ship docked in New York, union activist Bill Bailey (who would later fight for the Republic in the Spanish Civil War) took advantage of the gathered protesters to sneak on board and make a daring dash to the bow where he seized and ripped down the swastika it was displaying.[49] In England, 3000 fascists attempting to march into a Jewish area of the East End were met by ten times as many anti-fascists who successfully dispersed the gathering.[50] The working classes of Europe, it seemed, did not agree that fascism was a tolerable barrier to Bolshevism. Many of those who had stood, and fought, against fascism in Germany and Italy found themselves the victims of violent reprisals and fled into exile in the remaining democracies of Spain, France, and the UK.

By the time that the Nazis began making plans for a propaganda games in Berlin, Barcelona had spent years laying down the ground work of a cross-class and politically progressive sports movement. This popular sport movement had helped to define who Catalans were and how they interacted. It forged a unity which united Catalans at both the ballot box and the barricades. When the time came for the Popular Front to unite around sport, it only made sense to do so in Barcelona, where the ERC had built a nation around popular physical culture.

Soon Spain, and then Europe, would see this conflict play out in the most brutal and deadly war the world had ever seen. But first, the last desperate attempts had to be made to forge inter-national solidarity and mutual understating using peaceful means. Sport was, at the time, a relatively modern and new concept, and it seemed a perfectly fitting way to bind the world together in the cause of progress. Although the games, and their objective, were ultimately unsuccessful, through a study of the planning of the Barcelona Popular Olympics of 1936, we can better understand the world that might have been had fascism met with a more unified opposition from democracy.

NOTES

1. David A Steinberg, "The Workers' Sport Internationals 1920–28." *Journal of Contemporary History* 13, no. 2 (1978): 233–51.
2. Carles Santacana i, and Xavier Pujadas i Martí. *L'Altra Olimpíada, Barcelona'36: Esport, Societat i Política a Catalunya (1900–1936)*. Llibres de l'Índex, 1990; Xavier Pujadas, and Carles Santacana. *Història Il·lustrada de l'esport a Catalunya 1870–197*. Barcelona, 1995.
3. R. Brubaker, *Nationalist Politics and Everyday Ethnicity in a Transylvanian Town* (Princeton Univ Pr, 2006).
4. Pamela Beth Radcliff. 2017. *Modern Spain, 1808 to the Present*. First edition. A New History of Modern Europe 12. Hoboken, NJ: Wiley-Blackwell.
5. José Álvarez-Junco. 2011. *Spanish Identity in the Age of Nations*. Manchester University Press Manchester, England.
6. *Tierra y Libertad*, November 10, 1933.
7. Julián Casanova. *The Spanish Republic and Civil War*. Cambridge; New York: Cambridge University Press, 2010.

8. As did the conservative groups, but their support was of less consequence.
9. Carlos Jerez Farrán and Samuel Amago, eds., *Unearthing Franco's Legacy: Mass Graves and the Recovery of Historical Memory in Spain*, Contemporary European Politics and Society (Notre Dame, Ind: University of Notre Dame Press, 2010).
10. J Peirats., J. P. Valls, and C. Ealham. *The CNT in the Spanish Revolution.* Vol. 1. 3 vols. Meltzer Press, 2001.
11. A. Beevor, *The Battle for Spain: The Spanish Civil War, 1936–1939* (Penguin Group USA, 2006).
12. D. R Ringrose. 1998. *Spain, Europe, and the "Spanish Miracle", 1700–1900.* Cambridge Univ Pr.
13. Enric Ucelay-Da Cal. "History, Historiography and the Ambiguities of Catalan Nationalism." *Studies on National Movements*, Vol 1 (2013) (April 30, 2013).
14. E Weber. 1976. *Peasants into Frenchmen: The Modernization of Rural France, 1870–1914.* Stanford Univ Pr.
15. Benedict Anderson. 1983. *Imagined Communities: Reflections on the Origin and Spread of Nationalism.* Verso Books.
16. The Modernist school of nationalism studies has many proponents, but the work of Ernst Gellner makes a good starting point for the interested reader. Ernest Gellner and J. Breuilly. 2006. *Nations and Nationalism.* Blackwell Pub.
17. George Orwell. 1968. "The Sporting Spirit." *The Collected Essays, Journalism and Letters of George Orwell* 4:1945–50.
18. Eric Hobsbawm and Terence Ranger. *The Invention of Tradition.* Cambridge University Press, 2012.
19. Mike Cronin. *Sport and Nationalism in Ireland: Gaelic Games, Soccer, and Irish Identity since 1884.* Dublin, Ireland; Portland, OR: Four Courts Press, 1999.
20. C. L. R. James and R. Lipsyte, *Beyond a Boundary* (Duke Univ Pr, 1993).
21. C. S. Thompson, *The Tour de France: A Cultural History* (Univ of California Pr, 2008).
22. David Goldblatt, *The Games: A Global History of the Olympics* (WW Norton & Company, 2018).
23. Richard Gruneau, "'Amateurism' as a Sociological Problem: Some Reflections Inspired by Eric Dunning," Sport in Society 9, no. 4 (October 1, 2006): 559–82, https://doi.org/10.1080/17430430600768793.
24. Kuang Keng Keuk Ser, "See 120 Years of Struggle for Gender Equality at the Olympics," accessed September 4, 2018, https://www.pri.org/stories/2016-08-17/see-120-years-struggle-gender-equality-olympics.

25. B. J. Keys, *Globalizing Sport: National Rivalry and International Community in the 1930s* (Harvard Univ Pr, 2006).
26. David Goldblatt, *The Games: A Global History of the Olympics* (WW Norton & Company, 2018).
27. Will Rogers, "American Whites Will Come Into Own When Cocktailing Begins," *The Athens Messenger*, August 4, 1932.
28. Peter L. Dixon, *The Olympian* (Santa Monica, CA: New York: Roundtable Pub.; Distributed by Hippocrene Books, 1984).
29. Buzz Bissinger, "Stop the Games," *New York Times*, April 13, 2008.
30. Eduardo Vivancos, "Los Otros Juegos Olímpicos de Barcelona," accessed August 31, 2018, https://www.nodo50.org/esperanto/artik33es.htm.
31. Andrew McFarland. 2011. "The Importance of Reception: Explaining Sport's Success in Early Twentieth-Century Spain." *European Review* 19 (4): 527–43.
32. For examples of the existing historiography, see: Xavier Pujadas, *Catalunya i l'olimpisme*, 1st ed. (Barcelona: Coc Catalan, 2006); A. Gounot, "El Proyecto de La Olimpiada Popular de Barcelona (1936), Entre Comunismo Internacional y Republicanismo Regional," *Cultura, Ciencia y Deporte*, no. 3 (2005): 115; J. E. R. Hargreaves, *Freedom for Catalonia?: Catalan Nationalism, Spanish Identity, and the Barcelona Olympic Games* (Cambridge Univ Pr, 2000); Carles Santacana i Torres and Xavier Pujadas i Martí, *L'Altra Olimpíada, Barcelona'36: Esport, Societat i Política a Catalunya (1900–1936)* (Llibres de l'Índex, 1990); X. Pujadas and C. Santacana, "The Popular Olympic Games, Barcelona 1936: Olympians and Antifascists," *International Review for the Sociology of Sport* 27, no. 2 (1992): 139.
33. Brian Bunk. 2017. "Sport in an Authoritarian Regime: The Primo de Rivera Era in Spain, 1923–30." *Bulletin for Spanish and Portuguese Historical Studies* 42 (2), 92.
34. Xavier Pujadas and Carles Santacana. 2001. "La mercantilización del ocio deportivo en España. El caso del fútbol 1900–1928," *Historia Social* 44.
35. J. Burns, *Barça: A People's Passion* (Bloomsbury, 1999).
36. "FC Barcelona Statement," October 1, 2017. https://www.fcbarcelona.com/club/news/2017-2018/fc-barcelona-statement-1-october-las-palmas.
37. Brian Bunk. 2017. "Sport in an Authoritarian Regime: The Primo de Rivera Era in Spain, 1923–30." *Bulletin for Spanish and Portuguese Historical Studies* 42 (2), 92.
38. *La Rambla*, March 27, 1931.
39. See, for example, Jeroni Morages. "La Moral i La Natció." *Natació*, July 1933.

40. Fallon and Bell cite Cañardo's own re telling of this story to the publication *Dicen* in 1978 Lucy Fallon and Adrian Bell, *Viva La Vuelta!* (Norwich: Mousehold Press, 2005) pp. 20–21.

41. "Rugby." *La Vanguardia*, January 4, 1934.

42. A Gounot. "El Proyecto de La Olimpiada Popular de Barcelona (1936), Entre Comunismo Internacional y Republicanismo Regional." *Cultura, Ciencia y Deporte*, no. 3 (2005): 115.

43. Xavier Pujadas. "Sport, Ideology and Transnational Movements: The Case of the Relationship between the Czechoslovakian Sokols and the Catalan Popular Sports Movement (1912–1936)." Gorzow, POL, 2008.

44. International Olympic Committee, "Factsheet: The Games of the Olympiad," October 1, 2013.

45. COOP. "Manifest, Programa," 1936.

46. Maria Ginesta, the *miliciana* famously photographed by Juan Guzmán, had been a competitive hurdler earlier in the 1930s.

47. Julian Jackson. *The Popular Front in France: Defending Democracy 1934–38*. Cambridge: Cambridge Univ. Press, 1999.

48. Harry W. Laidler, *History of Socialism: An Historical Comparative Study of Socialism, Communism, Utopia* (Routledge, 2013).

49. Daniel Czitrom, "'Who the Hell Worked out a Plan like That?' New Light on the 1935 Bremen Riot," *The Volunteer*, February 27, 2018.

50. Tony Kushner and Nadia Valman, *Remembering Cable Street: Fascism and Anti-Fascism in British Society*, ed. Tony Kushner and Nadia Valman (Vallentine Mitchell, 1999), https://eprints.soton.ac.uk/397571/.

CHAPTER 2

The Berlin Games and the Boycott

Abstract Having established the background that made Catalonia uniquely suited to a celebration of cross-class sporting solidarity, this chapter establishes the specifics of the movement to boycott the Berlin games. Through examining the process which awarded the games to Berlin rather than to Barcelona and the ensuing political debates in pivotal nations (the USA, UK, Spain, and France), the chapter will show how the movement to boycott the Berlin games united various political groups who would not usually make common cause and provided a platform for the growth of the Popular Front and anti-fascism.

Keywords Olympics • Berlin • Barcelona • IOC • Avery Brundage • Pierre De Coubertin • Baillet-Latour • Jeremiah Mahoney

It was not at the April 1931 meeting of the International Olympic Committee (IOC) held in Barcelona that Berlin was awarded the games of the 11th Olympiad. Instead, a mail ballot due to poor attendance decided the venue of the 1936 games. Perhaps the fact that Spain's Second Republic had been declared just 12 days before unsettled many of the aristocrats[1] who would have been in attendance. A combination of the 19 votes counted at the session and 40 mail-in votes yielded a result of 43–16 (with 8 abstentions) in favour of awarding the games to Berlin.[2] At the time, both Spain and Germany were, politically at least, visions of the

J. Stout, *The Popular Front and the Barcelona 1936 Popular Olympics*, Mega Event Planning,
https://doi.org/10.1007/978-981-13-8071-6_2

future of a continent which had been torn apart by the war to end all wars and which had visions of a democratic century to follow the dynastic conflict of 1914–1918. A decade later, both Barcelona and Berlin would, once again, have heard the sound of gunfire and felt the pain of war.

The IOC awards Olympiads to cities, not states, and it had long been a project of the Catalan elites to bring the games to Barcelona. These well-connected and well-heeled Catalans were the initial impulse behind the 1913 founding of the *Comité Olímpic Català* (COC, Catalan Olympic Committee) a decade before its Spanish equivalent. The elites of Catalonia had long felt that their best route into the European elite was through culture, and many interpreted the Olympics as a perfect springboard to launch Barcelona higher on the world stage. Plans for a lavish stadium often appeared in the Catalan press, and various industrialists and clubs put forth different ideas for the structure to provide a sporting version of the Sagrada Família.[3] The first failed Catalan Olympic candidacy predated the Republic when the 1924 games were awarded to Paris, not Barcelona, at the request of the founder of the modern Olympics, Pierre de Coubertin.[4] In 1928, Catalan elites watched as the cornerstone to a huge stadium that formed part of an inter-national exposition was laid by Count Henri II de Baillet-Latour, the then president of the IOC. A year later, Catalonia hosted the exposition and placed sports at the forefront of the events. The same buildings would make the Popular Olympics possible, but the aristocratic Baillet-Latour would have nothing to do with them.

Despite this sustained campaign to bring the games to Barcelona, the IOC voted in favour of Berlin in 1931. Berlin had been set to hold the games in 1916, but the First World War put a stop to this and halted all German participation until 1928. By 1931, it was felt that the political environment of Spain's Second Republic was not stable enough to host the games and that (ironically) the Weimar regime in Germany at the time was a more suitable candidate. Although Catalan sports diplomacy seemed to have failed, it would turn out that the existing infrastructure and stable government would offer a chance for Barcelona to step into the gaps between the ideals of the Olympic movement and the Nazi party. In the five years between the awarding of the games to Berlin and their occurrence, Spain's Second Republic would see violence and reform, Catalonia would briefly proclaim itself an independent state within a federal republic, the Nazis would seize power in Germany, and the world would have to come to terms with the impending conflict between fascism and democracy in Europe.

THE NAZI GAMES

Berlin was awarded the games under the democratic Weimar regime, but the state's politics changed dramatically in March 1933. When the opening ceremony of the games took place in 1936, it was into a dictatorship, not a democracy, that the youth of the world marched. With the passage of the enabling act, Hitler swept away democracy and made the parliament a mere rubber stamp for his party-state, and with the state came the Olympic Games that were already being planned.

Nazi election material had been highly dismissive about the Olympic ideal, and it was presumed that the new regime would cancel the games.[5] However, Josef Goebbels was never one to forgo a propaganda opportunity and persuaded the regime to embrace the games as a chance to demonstrate Nazi efficiency and Aryan superiority. Just a week after their election, the Nazis called the organizers of the games to a meeting and shocked them by announcing they wished to continue with the events.

The Olympic bell in Berlin was inscribed with "I summon the youth of the world"; whilst this may have been the stated goal of the IOC's games, it was only a racial and politically circumscribed portion of that youth that was welcome at the *Olympiastadion* in Berlin. For a regime with its ideology embedded in an ethnonationalist myth and a eugenic future, the Olympic Games offered a perfect opportunity to prove its claims of a racial hierarchy and Nazi links to classical Greece. The explicit competition between nations at the Olympics, always popular in the US news media, was made part of the games in a more organized fashion after they fell under control of the Nazi propaganda machine. For the first time, a medal table was introduced, with the intention of proving the overall superiority of the Aryan nations. In the opening ceremony, many athletes from different nations gave the Nazi salute. The Olympic torch relay, a central element of today's sporting choreography with no real antecedent in classical civilization, was dreamed up by Dr. Carl Diemand and seized upon by Goebbels to forge closer links between Berlin and the classical roots of the games.[6] The Nazis solidified their propaganda coup with Leni Riefenstahl's film "Olympia" which used cinema as a tool for propaganda, showcasing the order and discipline behind the success of the Nazi games and glorifying the bodies of Aryan athletes. When *The New York Times* stated "no country since ancient Greece has displayed a more truly national interest in the Olympic spirit than you will find in Germany today,"[7] it did not fully realize the Nazi definition of nation and the exclusive fashion in which this interest was perceived.

THE BOYCOTT MOVEMENT

Before a flag was waved or a race run, the Berlin games had already gener-
ated their fair share of column inches. The IOC and many of its member
states repeatedly asked for, and received, assurances that Jewish athletes of
sufficient athletic ability would not be barred from the German team due
to their religion or ethnicity. These assurances had been given repeatedly,
but the regime in Berlin was not in the habit of keeping its promises.
Following the Winter Games of the same year, also hosted in Germany,
Hitler had remilitarized the Rhineland in direct contravention of the
Treaty of Versailles and begun a series of aggressions which would become
harder and harder for other governments to overlook.

The absence of Jewish athletes in German teams,[8] along with more general Nazi abuses of human rights and members of the opposition, caused a
stir in the press of more democratic nations around the world. For many, the
idea of taking part in a spectacle glorifying a regime that was becoming
increasingly genocidal was abhorrent, and there emerged a campaign to
boycott the Berlin games as a statement of opposition to the Nazi regime.
The Nazis were broad in their definition of enemies of the nation, and this
forced groups who were previously unfamiliar with each other into a unified
boycott movement. In many ways, the ideology behind boycott movements
and their growth through opposition to fascism paralleled that of the
Popular Front. In both cases, differences were cast aside as groups came
together to oppose the hatred and violence that fascism espoused.

Jewish people were being denied membership in private German sports
clubs by 1934, providing a de facto barrier to their being selected for the
Olympic team. A year later, they were denied German citizenship entirely.
Despite assurances that Jews would be able to compete, the Nazi team in
Berlin very much reflected the eugenic ideals of the regime. These ideals
were also reflected in the deep dis-ease that the Nazis felt about black
athletes competing with, and frequently defeating, their white counterparts. At least once it was suggested that after the impressive displays of
black Olympians in 1932, they should be barred from the 1936 games.[9]
Alongside the Jews, those on the political left in Germany also faced persecution, imprisonment, or worse. Thus, Germany, which had once hosted
the strongest Workers' Sports scene in the world, saw these organizations
supressed and many of their adherents imprisoned or in exile by the time
the games took place. As media reports of these, and other, Nazi repres-
sions and atrocities began to spread, so did global calls for a boycott.

As many governments would point out, it is not the government of a state but the National Organizing Committee that is represented at an Olympiad. However, the funding and the moral support of a government are vital for any Olympic team, let alone an event, especially one on the scale of the Berlin games. With this in mind, appeals were made to both sports organizers and politicians to leverage the Olympics in order to force the Nazi regime to respect the human rights of its citizens. These appeals met with mixed success. Keys argues that "small but significant"[10] concessions were made by the regime, but the inclusion of two athletes of mixed ancestry and temporary hiding of anti-Semitic propaganda don't seem all that significant when weighed against the continuing trend of dehumanizing hatred and eugenic propaganda. Attending the games, many argued, would constitute an implicit support of the Nazi regime. Meanwhile, not attending would, in the eyes of others, be an undue intrusion of politics into the realm of athletics that would harm the athletes much more than their hosts.

The USA

Following the 1932 games, the USA has unassailably laid claim to the leadership of the modern sporting movement—sport as spectacle had become an American industry. However, there was deep unease about the hosts of the games which followed those in Los Angeles. Opposition to the sending of a team to Berlin came from political groups as well as sporting organizations such as the Amateur Athletic Union (AAU) and the American Olympic Committee (AOC). Although the objections were at first legal in nature (discrimination on grounds of race and religion violated the Olympic Charter), it quickly became clear that rules far beyond those of the games were being broken. It was this moral objection that provided the foundation for a boycott movement that would see the Jewish political lobby, the National Association for the Advancement of Colored People (NAACP), and much of the political left make common cause.

The US boycott had a figurehead in Judge Jeremiah Mahoney, president of the Amateur Athletic Union. Mahoney was strongly opposed by the chair of the AOC, Avery Brundage.[11] Brundage hid behind the claim that "[t]he Olympic Games belong to the athletes and not to the politicians."[12] This "apolitical" positioning, of course, was, in itself, a highly political action and showed a support for the Nazi regime that, in his case, went beyond the implicit. Brundage may not have entered the debate as

an anti-Semite, but the combination of fierce opposition to the US attendance and the withdrawal of Jewish donations that nearly left the AOC
bankrupt seems to have turned him into one. He saw the boycott campaign as meddling in his private fiefdom and those who wished to take
sporting decisions away from him as more lamentable than the Nazis who
they opposed. Brundage was not alone in accepting a degree of anti-
Semitism that, while not genocidal, was certainly far from the equality
which the Olympic charter espoused. "I am not personally fond of jews
[sic] and of the jewish [sic] influence," IOC president Comte Henri de
Baillet-Latour wrote to Brundage, "but I will not have them molested in
no way [sic] whatsoever."[13]

Much of the conflict over the boycott in the USA can be seen through
the interpersonal conflict between Brundage and Mahoney and the organizations that they oversaw. Brundage liked to say revolutionaries were
not bred on the playing field, a neat encapsulation of his devotion to
defending the status quo and obeying the rules.[14] Mahoney meanwhile
was a Catholic judge and had political ambitions and fewer qualms about
using sport for social and political change. He authored a pamphlet out-
lining specific cases where Germany had broken the rules of the Olympic
Charter, all of which have been verified by subsequent research. With
Mahoney at its head, the AAU passed a resolution in favour of a boycott
in November 1933.[15]

For Brundage, the issue was that the boycott movement focused on
something more than the rules of the game. He saw the calls for a boycott
as essentially political attempts to undermine and attack the Nazi regime
and thus totally unacceptable in the sporting sphere. Brundage was not
wrong, and few on the boycott side would have denied that their goals
went beyond sport. But their disagreement with Brundage was regarding
whether sport should be considered entirely distinct from the political
realities of the day, or part of them. Brundage toured Germany's facilities
in 1934 and concluded that their programmes were in line with the
Olympic spirit. Perhaps because Brundage neither spoke German nor
spent time alone with the people he interviewed, this did little to calm the
boycott movement. The back and forth between these parties and the
IOC was published almost daily in the press[16] but largely ignored by
Roosevelt in the White House.[17] Over time, Brundage became the
staunchest opponent of the boycott campaign. The AOC chair actively
advocated for full attendance and went so far as to blame the boycott on
"a Jewish Communist conspiracy."[18]

As Brundage observed, "the Jews have been clever enough to realize the publicity value of sport,"[19] but they were far from unique. The boycott movement in the USA united a disparate number of groups who would go on to support the Popular Olympics in Barcelona. The NAACP and the political left also formed the rallying points of the boycott campaign. Despite the fact that writers never seem to tire of telling the story of Jesse Owens' four gold medals—three in individual events and one as part of a team—there has been little reflection on the black citizens of the USA who elected not to travel to a state that saw them as subhuman.[20] Prominent black newspapers encouraged Owens and others not to attend.[21] The newspaper *The New York Amsterdam News* wrote an open letter to Olympic athletes, offering them the "greatest opportunity"[22] of their careers "to challenge a force which seeks to destroy everything you have devoted your best years to building."[23] For many athletes, the opportunity offered was life changing. The chance to elevate oneself from a second-class citizen to a national hero and to be the actor and not the acted upon cannot have been an easy one to give up.

The NAACP opposed participation in the Berlin games, not only due to direct racism against black people by the Nazis,[24] but also in the interest of making common cause with the Jews. At first, it seemed that the boycott was an affront to the struggle of black people in the USA. Why complain about mistreatment of Jews in Germany when the USA had its own issues? Why protest the exclusion of Jewish athletes when the USA excluded black athletes from baseball and forced them to play in Negro Leagues? Certainly, if individual athletes were to boycott, shouldn't the black athletes go and use the platform they were given to disprove eugenic ideologies? However, solidarity in the face of persecution overcame all these arguments, and in July of 1933, the NAACP passed a resolution demanding that the USA's representatives at the IOC secure a guarantee on the part of the German government that discrimination on racial grounds would not be tolerated.[25]

In his correspondence, Brundage labelled the boycott movement as being created by "the well-disciplined forces of approximately 20 million Catholics and more than four million Jews."[26] He was not wrong about the involvement of the church, but this went beyond Catholics who could easily be demonized and marked as "other" given their relatively recent assimilation into whiteness in the USA. The Catholic publication *Commonweal* as well as an organization of Catholic veterans appealed for a boycott despite Brundage refusing to acknowledge that Catholic

Germans were in danger from the neopaganism of the Nazi regime.[27] Mahoney was also clearly troubled by this persecution and mentioned the neopaganism of the Nazi regime and its attacks on the Christian church in an open letter to the organizers of the games.[28] The more liberal wing of the Protestant church in the USA also took a principled stand against Nazism, with periodicals such as *The Christian Century* leading the way. One editorial referred to the Nazi press' anti-Semitism as "a symbol and a brand of shame upon the German government and people."[29] Another was more direct and personal in the apportion of blame, referring to Brundage as an "ecstatic nazi [sic] admirer."[30] By late 1935, with the national debate in full swing, organizations, including the Anti-Nazi League, the Anti-Defamation League, the American League Against War and Fascism, and even prominent Swedish-Americans began to support calls for a boycott, and a diverse coalition against the Berlin games began to take shape.

It was in December 1935 that the AAU decided, by a vote of 58¼ to 55¾, to send a team to Berlin.[31] Brundage would accompany the US team to Berlin, where he allegedly propositioned female athletes[32] and removed Jewish sprinters from the 4 × 100 m relay team.[33] Despite the incredible amount of planning, money, and work that went into crafting a spectacle of Aryan superiority, it would be black American athlete Jesse Owens who would grace the front covers of the newspapers reporting from Berlin, a significant shot across the bows of Hitler's racial hierarchy. Even the German fans, taken as they were with Owens' superhuman performances, would cheer the sprinter who grew up as the son of a sharecropper and grandson of a slave but became, briefly, the most recognizable athlete in the world.

On 15–16 August, the last two days of the Berlin games, 7500 people watched the "World Labor Athletic Carnival" on New York's Randall's Island.[34] This hugely successful event was organized by the AAU and the Jewish Labour Committee. Even after the team had left for Berlin, members of the anti-boycott lobby attempted to stop the AAU name being associated with an alternative event. However, unlike the Barcelona Popular Olympics, the carnival did not seek to challenge the authority of the Berlin Olympics. The Labor Carnival was supplementary and did not take the name "Olympic." The Carnival did not tempt athletes away from the games, nor did it take the form of a real alternative. The carnival followed in the footsteps of the Workers' Olympics in being open to a limited pool of participants who were already ideologically homogeneous. Such events reinforced existing identities rather than taking advantage of the ability of such an event to create new identities and build bridges between existing ones. However, this was not the only manifestation of opposition to the events in Berlin. A ship had sailed from the East Coast to carry a delegation of athletes to the Popular Olympics in Barcelona the month before, adding valuable inter-national support to their claims of being the true manifestation of the Olympic Spirit.

FRANCE

France stood, both literally and metaphorically, between the Berlin and Barcelona games, and the nation, with its young government, was torn between the two Olympiads. In December 1935, when a socialist deputy introduced a bill that moved to stop the 900,000-Franc payment that was to be made to train and equip French Olympic teams, it was defeated 410–151.[35] This defeat reflected the distinct divide between the elite or bourgeois sport that would have been represented at the Olympics, and Workers' Sport which was largely represented at Spartakiads and Workers' Olympics. These two tendencies did not meet, compete, or even agree on very much. It was to be the role of the Popular Front government in France, and the popular games in Barcelona, to try to bring these two tendencies together in opposition to fascism.

Perspectives on sport in France at the time reflected the different world-views of the athletes involved. Both bourgeois and working-class sports organizations served to create and cement social ties between their adherents and build barriers to those in the other organizations. French workers flocked to the Workers' Sport movement and, as geographically and ideologically close as they found themselves to their German comrades, tended to support the boycott in solidarity with those who faced persecution for their race or politics in fascist Germany. In 1934, the FSGT (*Fédération Sportive et Gymnique du Travail*—Workers' Sporting and Gymnastic Federation) had been formed to unify communist and socialist sporting bodies in a single popular sporting organization to enhance this solidarity in the face of threat. That same year sporting events were organized to oppose "war and fascism" by the new organization.[36]

Whilst a minority of France's bourgeoisie may have preferred the Third Reich to the Popular Front, many more could not be convinced of the benefits of a boycott even if they disagreed with the regime in Berlin. Bourgeois sports held that sport and politics could be kept apart, an easier position to hold if one finds oneself at the top of the proverbial ladder in one's society. Workers and bourgeois sports associations agreed on very little and rarely met on the field of play; the boycott of the 1936 games was not any less divisive.

Both the political and sporting worlds that these two groups inhabited would come together in opposition to fascism in May 1936 with the election of a Popular Front government composed of the French communist, radical, socialist, and workers' parties. In the context of a leftist government that explicitly opposed fascism, it seemed absurd for the government to fund the sons and daughters of the wealthiest citizens in their mediocre achievements under the watchful eyes of their Nazi neighbours.

The *Comité International pour le Respect de l'Espirit Olympique* (CIREO) was formed in Paris in April 1936 and contained representatives from around Europe. Although it seems to have shared space with the Red Sports International (RSI), it welcomed a broader range of participants in the spirit of the Popular Front.[37] The CIREO issued a circular informing artists, activists, and athletes of the conference it planned to hold in June of that same year. In the crowd sat a joint Catalan-Spanish delegation containing many of the executive board of the committee that would organize the Popular Olympics. Alongside the Catalans sat "representatives of Switzerland, Holland, France, Norway, Sweden, Denmark, England and Czechoslovakia," and they were "unanimously of the opinion that the People's Olympiad at Barcelona was the greatest sporting event of the year and the surest demonstration against the Olympic games in Berlin."[38] At that meeting, the keynote speech was delivered by Heinrich Mann, Thomas Mann's brother. Mann railed against those who would attend the Berlin games and urged the newly elected premier to confront the issue, stating "he who goes to Berlin deserts the Popular Front."[39]

Blum did not take up Mann's suggestion. Amidst a wave of occupations and strikes, the Jewish premier feared a total boycott of the games in Berlin would fatally discredit his young government, add to anti-Semitic conspiracy theories, and perhaps prove fatal to his fragile hold on power. The French government cited the precedent set by attending the 1936 Winter Games and opted to send a team to Berlin and Barcelona. France sent a team of 150 athletes to Berlin, a reduction from the 255 who had been planning on attending. The budget was trimmed from 1,895,000 to 1,000,000 Francs.[40]

With the traditionally dominant USA and the Popular Front government of France not willing to lead boycott efforts, the possibility of a failed Berlin games seemed scant. Nevertheless, Catalonia provided an opportunity for individuals and groups who chose not to go to Berlin to show their unity.

THE UK

British politics in the 1930s flirted with both extremes of the political spectrum, and the debate around the games largely settled upon the well-drawn divisions between classes and ideologies. British Conservatives, fearful of a conflict as destructive as the First World War, executed a succession of logical and moral gymnastics that were Olympian in their complexity in order to justify appeasing the Nazi regime. Part of this routine was the mobilization of a distinction between sport and politics that allowed British politicians to look the other way whilst atrocities were committed in Germany.

The British Non-Sectarian Anti-Nazi Council campaigned for a boycott of Nazi Germany that went beyond the Olympics; they were joined by the Trades Union Congress whose General Secretary, Sir Walter Citrine, was a signatory to the CIREO documents circulated after the conference in Paris.[41] Public awareness of the boycott movement began when England's football team were to play Germany at Tottenham's stadium. The London club had many Jewish fans and the stadium was located in the heart of a Jewish community. The game was met with protests and unrest; it was clear that there would not be any British civility for the Nazi regime's representatives amongst the Spurs fans who gathered to oppose the German team that day. On the same date as the game, an article in the Manchester *Guardian* addressed the Olympic issue, stating that "if Germany today has no Jews of Olympic caliber it is because she has denied them adequate facilities for training and competition and has forced them into exile or suicide."[42]

The British Cabinet seems to have been rather torn on the issue. Great attention was paid to the movement of the boycott in the USA[43] and the "German keenness not to offend Americans,"[44] further illustration of Keys' claim that the Olympic movement was closely associated with the USA in the period. Minutes of meetings reveal that they found themselves in "a rather delicate position," but it was felt that "it is nowhere suggested that the withdrawal of the British team would wreck the games. Finally, it does not seem clear that if the games were wrecked the Jews would necessarily be any better off—probably the reverse—so that our action, if successful, would fail to achieve its ostensible object." Annotations to the telegrams sent from the British ambassador to Germany reveal the infighting in the Foreign Office, intelligence officer Ralph Wigram (who would die in suspicious circumstances in 1936[45]) seemingly advocating for more leverage to be exercised while others suggested "we had better stay out of all that," with another noting "we certainly ought to see if we can't use this a lever."[46]

The language used in Foreign Office meetings suggests that, whatever their public position might be, the ministers in question were well aware that sport could be used to make a political statement; the question was what statement they wished to make. Ultimately, it was decided that boycotting the Olympics would not help the cause of German Jews, or at least not help the British Empire in its relations with Germany. Perhaps more pragmatic considerations came into play when the British government realized that any boycott without the USA involved would leave Britain embarrassed as Hitler's party went on across the channel without British guests.

SPAIN

Spain elected a Popular Front government in February 1936. Indeed, the Spanish general election coincided with the closing ceremony of the Winter Olympic Games at Garmisch-Partenkirchen, where Spanish athletes had been assaulted on suspicion of being Jews.[47] Spain had seen the possibility for political violence stemming from ideological disagreement in 1934; it surely knew what was at stake with the appeasement of fascism, and the question of the games soon arose. This issue was debated for some time in front of Premier Miguel Azaña before he finally made his decision on June 28, 1936. It was decided that the Spanish state would not fund teams attending the Berlin games.[48]

It was not just the government in Spain who could fund teams in Berlin. Even when Azaña opted not to fund Spanish participation, the Spanish Olympic Committee had other ideas.[49] They intended to send athletes to Berlin in 12 events[50] and, in a speech given in response to the government decision to boycott the Games, praised the games as a "manifestation of … human fraternity"[51] and elected to support teams. Other national federations and private groups offered to pay the way of their athletes to Berlin. Just a year before, Spanish football players had given the Republican salute after winning a game in Cologne; perhaps some hoped they could do the same in Berlin. This left Palestine as the sole National Olympic Committee which elected to refuse the invitation to compete in Berlin.

It is sad to note that these games would be, in a sense, the beginning of the end of the Spanish Republic. It was from the Olympic Village that was built for the Games in Berlin that the Condor Legion, a secret air force unit that aided Franco in his coup, departed in 1936. Before the village was used to hold athletes, it had been used to house and train this clandestine unit, which would later bomb Guernica and play a pivotal role in the defeat of the Republic.[52]

THE CATALAN GAMES

The problem with boycotts is that they are largely invisible. One cannot see the crowds of people who are not attending an event, just those who are. Without a central gathering place, the Berlin boycott risked being just another invisible protest. The individuals who elected not to go would remain isolated at home, while those who picked sport over solidarity would be on the front cover of every newspaper in the world.

It was the Catalan government that stepped in to make this invisible boycott visible and to manifest unity where Berlin would seek to demonstrate difference. Barbara Keys, in her study of the 1932 and 1936 games, illustrates sport's "peculiar potency as a means of mediating between national and international identities,"[53] and it was this emerging property of inter-national sport that spurred the Popular Front to host an alternative to the games of Berlin. The event wouldn't have anywhere near as long as Berlin had to plan and prepare, but Catalonia's previous bids, experience hosting the exposition of 1929, and existing infrastructure would make it easy to put together an event in short order.

With a desire to host an alternative to the games prevalent across the Popular Front, as evidenced by the attendees at the CIREO meeting, the question was who could host them. The Workers' Sport associations had burned bridges with inter-national elite and bourgeois sporting bodies and thus were not capable of unifying all aspects of the boycott movement. Instead, a progressive organization without links to Moscow was required. As Pujadas and Santacana conclude, "There were few bodies and organizations with these characteristics in the thirties, when the world was split between fascism and communism. There were a few North American organizations, the Czechs with their Sokols, and the Catalans of the left."[54] The USA was too far away from the centre of the boycott movement, and the Sokols remained largely focused on their form of mass physical culture and not on the Olympic sports. This left the Catalans as the willing and capable hosts of the anti-fascist Olympiad.

Ideological opposition to the Berlin games abounded with the *Ateneu Enciclopedic Popular* (AEP), a Catalan cross-class group focused on popular education and sport, declaring the Nazi games "as good as dead" in April 1936, and the Ateneu, along with the Catalan press, took up the slogan "the Olympic Spirit is not in Berlin but in Barcelona."[55] At the end of that same month, the ERC and civil society came together to establish the *Comité Organitzador de l'Olimpíada Popular* (Committee for the Popular Olympic Games/COOP); with Catalan hero and president Lluís Companys himself as titular chairperson, an Executive Committee for the COOP followed on May 19. Josep Antoni Trabal,[56] who had been closely linked to the world of sport for over a decade and had led calls for popular sport even when the Olympics and stadia were mostly the interest of Catalonia's elites, chaired the committee. Jaume Miravitlles (an ex-communist, member of the ERC, and prolific author, journalist, and film producer) and Pere Aznar (president of the *Centre Autonomista de Dependents del Comerç i de la Indústria* [CADCI] trade union and a parliamentary representative of the *Partit Català Proletari* or Catalan Proletarian Party) served as the committee's vice-presidents. The rest of the committee included journalists and previous members of the CCEP. They would oversee a new kind of inter-national sporting event that would combine all classes and abilities and stand as an example of the cross-class physical culture that the ERC and its civil society allies aimed to create in Catalonia. This conscious placing of the Catalan nation into a progressive European narrative was a major and consistent part of the ERC's foreign policy and of Catalan identity.

A direct comparison of Berlin and Barcelona's games seems unjust and would reflect poorly on the Popular Olympics. However, the ideologies at play deserve comparison. The Popular Olympics of 1936 were to be a fraternal competition among brother nations, not a celebration of the superiority of one race or state (as in Berlin) or of one ideology (as was the case for the Workers' Games). Catalan newspaper *L'Acció*, on the eve of the Popular Olympics, made mention of "confronting" the Berlin games in its article, which went under the title of "Sport and Citizenship." They claimed that the Catalan games were designed to "create a sporting movement" rather than a spectacle and that "The diverse athletes from around the world who will be hosted in Catalonia these next few days will return home knowing how things should be done."[57] Many publications made explicit reference to the Berlin games and contrasted their outlook to those in Barcelona. The Popular Olympics were not a regularly scheduled ideological event like the Workers' Olympics. Instead, Barcelona's games were a rapidly organized response which attempted to use sport to support the Popular Front's inclusive narrative just as the Nazis had attempted to use sport to support their exclusive one.

The Barcelona games aimed to not only oppose the "disgraceful sham" in Berlin but also to promote "the brother-hood of all men and races" and also "[promote] the general development of popular sport."[58] In one press release, the games painted itself as an event in the "defense of human freedom, culture and progress."[59] This would include gender equality— women would be taking an increasing role in these games "not as a way of making a spectacle but to sow the seed of a genuine popular sport."[60] Athletes of all abilities would be welcome, and the programme for the games was explicit in stating that the Popular Olympics did not strive for the "production of sensational stars" but rather it aimed to give "impetus to progress and culture." This was, according to the organizers, a task well suited to the Catalans. Catalonia had "struggled heroically for centuries against social and national oppression" and would "welcome the representatives of the toilers of other countries and unite with them in a solemn undertaking to always maintain the true Olympic spirit, fighting for the brotherhood of men and of peoples, for progress, freedom and peace."[61]

CONCLUSIONS

Ultimately, the boycott lived and died by the actions of the USA. If the USA, which had taken nearly three times as many medals as its closest rival at the previous Olympic Games,[62] had decided to skip the games, they would have been joined by many of the other nations who held their own internal debates. It was Brundage's growing anti-Semitism, his feeling that the Nazis stood up to communism, and his conviction that sport was for the athletes, not the politicians (even when who those athletes could be was decided by politicians), that made the 1936 Olympics in Berlin possible. By making the Berlin games possible, Brundage made the Popular Olympics in Barcelona necessary.

This desire on the part of bourgeois legislators around the world to confront communism, combined with a distinct indifference towards the persecution of Jewish people in Germany, would go far beyond the sporting sphere. It was this same cocktail of hatred and indifference that would allow Hitler and the Nazis to grow stronger in the years between 1936 and 1939. This was the perspective that informed non-intervention in the Spanish Civil War even after the Condor Legion bombed civilians at Guernica. Brundage, who would later receive a contract to build the German embassy in the USA and campaigned to keep the USA out of the war until Pearl Harbor, would go on to serve as president of the IOC, where he would employ the same myopic dedication to the outdated ideal of amateurism as he did to the goal of allowing the Nazis their biggest propaganda coup. Blum would be arrested and sent to Buchenwald and then Dachau before orders for his execution were ignored and he was eventually liberated in May 1945. Azaña died in France in 1940, having seen his government and his country destroyed by the same indifference that allowed the Berlin games to proceed. Companys died at Montjuïc castle when a firing squad carried out the sentence of his trial, which had lasted less than one hour. Companys refused to wear a blindfold, and as he died, he could have almost seen the stadium that he would help refit for the popular games as it was just metres away from the castle walls. Despite the voluntarism, conviction, and bravery of those who stood up to Berlin and put on a games in Barcelona, they would end up much like their nascent Olympiad, as a footnote to European history amongst the thousands of other individuals and causes who fell victim to fascism and the indifference displayed to it.

Notes

1. The committee included five counts and one marquis.
2. "International Olympic Committee. Meeting of 1931 (Fourth Year of the Ninth Olympiad). Barcelona, 25th–26th April." Bulletin Officiel Du Comité International Olympique 18 (July 1931).
3. *Vanguardia*, December 5, 1914.
   La Vanguardia, July 6, 1917.
4. David Goldblatt, *The Games: A Global History of the Olympics* (WW Norton & Company, 2018).
5. *Los Angeles Times*, January 8, 1932.
6. Diem was not himself a Nazi; indeed, his wife was from a Jewish family. However, he had been integral to the securing of the games for Berlin before the Nazi takeover of power. He retained his position as secretary general of the Organizing Committee even after the regime change. Dr. Thomas Lewals, an equally experienced sports administrator, was removed

as president of the German Olympic Committee on account of his Jewish heritage.

7. *The New York Times,* October 5, 1936, quoted in Kanin, D. B. A *Political History of the Olympic Games.* Westview Pr, 1981.

8. One athlete who would have been legally considered half-Jewish (Mischling) under German law was allowed to compete. Helene Mayer, one of the greatest fencing athletes of all time, had a Jewish father and was permitted to compete for Germany. She won a silver medal and gave the Nazi salute on the podium.

9. David Goldblatt, *The Games: A Global History of the Olympics* (WW Norton & Company, 2018).

10. B. J. Keys, *Globalizing Sport: National Rivalry and International Community in the 1930s* (Harvard Univ Pr, 2006). Pp. 87

11. Brundage went on to chair the IOC where he would condemn the 1968 Black Power salute as "the nasty demonstration against the American flag by negroes." Guttmann, A. 2002. *The Olympics, a History of the Modern Games.* Univ of Illinois Pr, pp. 245.

12. Avery Brundage. *Fair Play for American Athletes.* American Olympic committee, 1934.

13. Carolyn Marvin, "Avery Brundage and American Participation in the 1936 Olympic Games," *Journal of American Studies,* 16, no. 1 (April 1982). Pp. 7.

14. Carolyn Marvin, "Avery Brundage and American Participation in the 1936 Olympic Games," *Journal of American Studies,* 16, no. 1 (April 1982).

15. *The New York Times November* 21, 1933.

16. For example, see *The New York Times* December 4 and 7, 1935.

17. Stephen R Wenn. 1991. "A Suitable Policy of Neutrality? FDR and the Question of American Participation in the 1936 Olympics." *The International Journal of the History of Sport* 8 (3):319–35.

18. Brundage once noted that he himself was a member of a sports club where Jews were not permitted to be members. Keys, B. J. *The dictatorship of sport: nationalism, internationalism, and mass culture in the 1930's: a thesis presented at Harvard University.*

19. Carolyn Marvin. "Avery Brundage and American Participation in the 1936 Olympic Games." Journal of American Studies, 16, no. 1 (April 1982). Pp. 8

20. German Newspapers such as *Volkischer Beobachter* had suggested that, after the 1932 games, it was important to exclude black participants Wiggins, David K. 1983. "The 1936 Olympic Games in Berlin: The Response of America's Black Press." *Research Quarterly for Exercise and Sport* 54 (3):278–92.

21. David K Wiggins. 1983. "The 1936 Olympic Games in Berlin: The Response of America's Black Press." *Research Quarterly for Exercise and Sport* 54 (3):278–92.

22. *The New York Amsterdam News* Aug 24, 1935 pp1; ProQuest Historical Newspapers New York Amsterdam News: 1922–1993.

23. *The New York Amsterdam News* Aug 24, 1935 pp1; ProQuest Historical Newspapers New York Amsterdam News: 1922–1993.

24. Although there were very clear attempts to prevent the undermining of eugenic arguments by black athletes, basketball players were limited to a maximum height, for instance, Holmes, J. Olympiad 1936: blaze of glory for Hitler's Reich. Ballantine Books.

25. Baltimore Afro-American October 21, 1933.

26. Carolyn Marvin. "Avery Brundage and American Participation in the 1936 Olympic Games." Journal of American Studies, 16, no. 1 (April 1982). Pp. 13.

27. Allen Guttmann. *The Games Must Go on: Avery Brundage and the Olympic Movement.* New York: Columbia University Press, 1984. Pp. 72.

28. The letter is included in a telegram from the British embassy in Washington to the British Foreign Secretary. Osborne, Francis D'Arcy. "Letter from Sir Francis D'Arcy Godolphin Osborne, Minister at the British Embassy in Washington to Sir Samuel Hoare, the Foreign Secretary," October 25, 1935. National Archive.

29. Eddy Sherwood. "Germany in Olympic Dress." *The Christian Century,* September 2, 1936.

30. The Christian Century, October 14, Volume XII-2003, 1936, p. 1347.

31. "AAU Votes for Full Olympic Game Participation to End 3-Day Debate," *Democrat and Chronicle,* December 9, 1935.

32. David Maraniss. *Rome 1960: The Olympics That Changed the World.* 1st Simon & Schuster hardcover ed. New York: Simon & Schuster, 2008.

33. David Clay Large. *Nazi Games: The Olympics of 1936.* 1st ed. New York: W.W. Norton, 2007.

34. Edward S. Shapiro, "The World Labor Athletic Carnival of 1936: An American Anti-Nazi Protest," *American Jewish History* 74, no. 3 (1985): 255–273.

35. Bruce Kidd. 1980. "The Popular Front and the 1936 Olympics." *Canadian Journal of the History of Sport and Physical Education* 11 (1): 1–18.

36. *Sport,* December 5, 1934.

37. A Gounot. "El Proyecto de La Olimpiada Popular de Barcelona (1936), Entre Comunismo Internacional y Republicanismo Regional." *Cultura, Ciencia y Deporte,* no. 3 (2005): 115.

38. COOP, "Press Service. English Edition, No. 5," June 1, 1936.

39. David Clay Large. *Nazi Games: The Olympics of 1936.* 1st ed. New York: W.W. Norton, 2007, 151.

40. COOP, "Press Service. English Edition, No. 6," June 18, 1936.

41. COOP, "Letter to Sir Walter Citrine, Secretary, Trades Union Congress General Council," June 18, 1936, Archives of the Trades Union Congress.

42. EA Montague. *Manchester Guardian*, December 5, 1935 as quoted in Paul A. Spencer, "A Discussion of Appeasement and Sport as Seen in the Manchester Guardian and the Times," Australian Society for Sports History Bulletin 2 (1996): 3–19.

43. Francis D'Arcy Osborne. "Letter from Sir Francis D'Arcy Godolphin Osborne, Minister at the British Embassy in Washington to Sir Samuel Hoare, the Foreign Secretary," October 25, 1935. National Archive.

44. Edward Phillips. "Telegram from Sir Edward Phillips," November 7, 1935.

45. Wigram was one of the first in the Foreign Office to raise the alarm about Nazi Rearmament. He died in late 1936, with the cause of death listed as "pulmonary embolism." A letter from Winston Churchill suggests he died in the arms of his wife, but others have suggested suicide. His family did not attend his funeral, lending some credibility to this theory.

46. Edward Phillips. "Telegram from Sir Edward Phillips, British Ambassador to Germany and minutes of subsequent meeting" November 11, 1935. National Archive and Edward Phillips. "Telegram from Sir Edward Phillips," November 7, 1935.

47. David Clay Large. *Nazi Games: The Olympics of 1936*. 1st ed. New York: W.W. Norton, 2007.

48. "El Estado Niega Toda Subvencion a La Participacion de Espana En Los Juegos Olimpicos." ABC. June 28, 1936.

49. "Los Espanoles Concurrian a Los Juegos de Berlin." ABC, July 5, 1936.

50. ABC, July 4th 1936.

51. "El Estado Niega Toda Subvencion a La Participacion de Espana En Los Juegos Olimpicos." ABC. June 28, 1936.

52. William Baker, "New Light on the Nazi Olympics," *Journal of Sport History* 8 (1981).

53. B. J Keys. 2006. *Globalizing Sport: National Rivalry and International Community in the 1930s*. Harvard Univ Pr.

54. X. Pujadas and C. Santacana, "The Popular Olympic Games, Barcelona 1936: Olympians and Antifascists," *International Review for the Sociology of Sport* 27, no. 2 (1992): 142.

55. AEP, "Berlin Una Altra Vega," *Butlleti D'Informacio De La Seccio De Gimnas i D'Esports De L'Ateneu Enciclopedic Popular*, April 1936.

56. Among other positions, he had served as director of the Catalan Athletics Federation and editor of sports publications including *La Jornada Deportiva*, *La Raça*, and *Sports*.

57. "Esport I Ciutadania." *l'Acció*. July 11, 1936.

58. COOP. "Manifest, Programa," 1936.

59. "Press Service. English Edition, No. 6," June 18, 1936. Archives of the Trades Union Congress.
60. "Esport I Ciutadania." *l'Acció.* July 11, 1936.
61. COOP. "Manifest, Programa," 1936.
62. David Goldblatt, *The Games: A Global History of the Olympics* (WW Norton & Company, 2018).

CHAPTER 3

Funding and Organizing an Alternative

Abstract This chapter looks at the mechanics of how Catalonia was able to not only organize but also pay for such a huge event in such a short period of time. Through tracing reported donations and fundraising as well as the formation of various organizing bodies, this chapter illustrates the importance of a national popular sporting infrastructure and an international Popular Front in creating a games which placed Catalonia on an equal footing with nation states, thanks to the inter-national coalition behind it.

Keywords Poster art • Popular Front • 1936 • Leon Blum • Spanish Civil War • Spanish Second Republic

The Spanish Second Republic and Civil War offer some of the most beautiful poster art of the twentieth century. Years ago, as an undergraduate in a library, it was these posters that first alerted me to the existence of the Popular Olympics. Now that same poster hangs on my office wall and offers a unique insight into the way the organizers of the Popular Olympics saw their event. The poster (Fig. 3.1) is an abstract representation of three men: one red-skinned, one black, and one yellow. Together, the men hold a flag bearing the words "Olimpiada Popular," and below them is the flag of Barcelona and the dates of the games (which were clearly amended just

© The Author(s) 2020

J. Stout, *The Popular Front and the Barcelona 1936 Popular Olympics*, Mega Event Planning,
https://doi.org/10.1007/978-981-13-8071-6_3

Fig. 3.1 Publicity poster showing the extended dates—Fritz Lewy

before going to print, as both the old dates and an additional panel with the new dates are visible). The COOP has its name printed on the bottom along with its office location at a trade union office in Barcelona. This early poster began life as a postage stamp and went through several itera-tions as the date range of the games was extended. It was designed by Fritz Lewy, himself emblematic of the games as a German Jewish exile living in Catalonia.[1] Later posters, which displayed the final dates (Fig. 3.2), included women in the front line of marching athletes and showed black, white, and Asian men and women marching together under the banner of the Olimpiada Popular. This poster art tells the reader most of what they

Fig. 3.2 Poster showing the participation of various races

needed to know about the games, that they were to embrace diversity and that everyone was welcome, that the games celebrated popular sport, workers' organizations, and the city of Barcelona, and that they were rushed in their planning and organization.

The Popular Olympics were, in every sense, the antithesis of the Berlin games. The Berlin poster (Fig. 3.3) shows a single muscular man, wearing the laurel wreath of a Greek Olympic champion. Beneath him a chariot is visible, pulled by four horses and carrying a person, and a symbol that appears to be the *Reichsadler*, the German imperial eagle. Unlike the Catalan games, this poster shows national pride, the symbols of the state

Fig. 3.3 Poster for the
Berlin Olympics

and of conquest, not of competition. Undoubtedly, the regime in Berlin
aimed to use the Berlin games to illustrate that they were physically and
logistically leaps and bounds ahead of the rest of Europe and saw themselves as the inheritors of the tradition of classical empire. The Olympiad
would serve as an illustration of their superiority in a thinly veiled threat
that armed conflict could only result in a victory for Hitler's regime.

The differences went much beyond their artistic expression. Berlin's
games offered an unprecedented scale of budget and government support.
The events at Berlin cost more than every other previous Olympiad combined and would transform the city into a film set that was articulated
towards the rest of the world, not to the competitors and spectators in the

stadium.[2] They would project discipline, order, strength, and the undeniable totalitarian power of the fascist state. Where the Berlin games were funded entirely by the Nazi regime as a propaganda spectacle, the Catalan games were not funded by or intended for the glorification of Catalonia or Spain. The Popular Olympics intended to facilitate the assembly of people from all over the world who would not only participate in the games, but also pay for them. The Popular Olympics were not designed to alter how the world saw Catalonia so much as to change how participants saw the world. Where there was a message, it was not about Catalonia's, or any other nation's, greatness but about the power that came from inter-national fraternity. The Popular Olympics aimed to give a youthful and muscular image to anti-fascism and show how the working people of the world could unite against hatred and scapegoating. The goal was that the people who came to Barcelona would come to see and experience solidarity between races and classes and then take that home. They did, but the experience came in the streets and not the stadium.

Such an event could not have been imagined without the ideological framework of the Popular Front and relied on opposition to fascism to bring athletes from around the globe. The Popular Olympiad was an international affair comprised of and funded by governments, unions, and civil society groups from around Europe as a performance of the solidarity and strength of the Popular Front against fascism. Andres Martin, head of the FCDO, a member of the committee of the RSI, and a member of the COOP, outlined that all except fascists were welcome in Barcelona, writing "clearly this is a Popular Games: that is to say of the people and for the people, and in which, therefore, fascists have no place, having shown themselves to be enemies of popular culture."[3] The events existed outside of the Workers' Sport network of which Martin was a part, even if it used many of the connections forged through the Marxist sporting sphere. Despite the absence of funding or competitors from the USSR, it was a policy from Moscow allowed for a network that was powerful enough to host an alternative game to come together in opposition to Berlin.

Catalonia had in place the sporting infrastructure required; this would save a huge amount of time and money compared to the model for IOC games which was moving towards what Andranovich et al. have termed "flipping the city."[4] Barcelona would reuse buildings from the 1929 Exposition and rely on the civil society and popular sport groups to host events and spectators. Catalonia also had a clear grasp of the popular sport movement's deep roots in civil society as well as government, meaning that it could call upon all the logistical and organizational resources which other nations had to construct around the Olympics. Multisport organizations and contests were a key part of the popular sport programme, and this made organizing easier compared to dealing with dozens of individuals sports federations as would have been the case in other polities. Most importantly though, Catalonia had an established success in using sport to create cross-class identities and a government and population determined to stand up to fascism.

Thus, Barcelona seemed the natural place to host the games. What was not so obvious was how to pay for an Olympiad, much less how to do so in a few months. For all the enthusiasm Catalonia had for popular sport, the ERC was far from capable of shouldering the costs of such an undertaking. The organizers expected 10,000 participants to march through the streets of Barcelona on the 19th of July, many more than would be seen in Berlin.[5] Many of them would need to have their travel funded and food and lodging provided. This was an almost unfathomable undertaking for a city that had just months to prepare, financial problems of its own, and no clear idea of what to expect in terms of attendance until just days before the events began. However, as the world would see in 1936, the Catalan Popular Front wasn't one to back away from a battle because the odds were not in its favour.

The funding of these games, which was markedly different from both the IOC games and the Workers' Sports events, illustrates the value placed on the Popular Olympics by the entire Popular Front and associated civil society groups. A manifestation of sporting unity would help to create an image of a Popular Front that existed outside of the halls of politics and was composed of young, healthy, and diverse people who would carry the flag of anti-fascism and the hopes of all of those who opposed what fascism stood for. It was through inter-national cooperation and support that the Popular Olympics were able to come together. The combination of supernational, national, and subnational actors is what gave strength to the Popular Front, and these games were to be an illustration of that.

Civil Society

Officially, the Popular Olympics were convened by the COOP. However, the events were, as *L'Acció* put it, "a collaboration of all the sporting, artistic and cultural organizations... [in association with] the ERC."[6] As the organizing committee noted in June, "As in Spain, so in all countries the Peoples' Olympiad has aroused the enthusiasm of thousands upon thousands of freedom-loving athletes. Only material difficulties prevent the flooding of Barcelona by the foreign delegation. Everywhere Peoples' Olympiad Committees are formed to organize the delegations. Clubs, groups and organizations join these committees in large numbers."[7] Just as the popular sport movement before the games had been a public-private partnership, so were the games themselves. The COOP itself contained both civil society and government officials and was based in the building of the *CADCI*, a Catalanist shop stewards trade union known as the *saltataulells* (counter-jumpers) and one of the key forces behind the diffusion of the Catalan language and identity beyond elites in the early twentieth century.

The COOP came into existence in April 1936, but its composition and ideology drew closely on the *Comité Català pro Esport Popular* (CCEP) which had been officially convened earlier in 1936[8] and often also met at the CADCI offices. Although the CCEP was not affiliated with any political party, it was very much a creation of the ERC's popular sport and physical education initiatives. It was consulted, formed, and funded by the Catalan government and contained many of the same personnel as the ERC's other sporting initiatives. The committee combined physical educators from the *Acadèmia d'Educació Física de Catalunya* (AEFC) as well as the architects of the nation's sporting infrastructure, theorists who wrote on physical culture in organizations of the Catalan sports movement such as the *AEP*, CADCI, the *Club Femeni i d'Esports*, and the *Centre Gimnastic Barcelones*. The organization, which *Mundo Deportivo* described as having "the air of a soviet," aimed to "popularize sport as a form of culture and physical regeneration [for the nation]."[9] These bodies would also steer participants away from the excesses of elite sport which one member described as "fists and feet used with mal intent."[10]

The COOP formed its executive committee on May 19, 1936,[11] and counted many of the founding figures of popular sport from both government and civil society amongst its members. Josep Antoni Trabal, who had been closely linked to the world of popular sport for over a decade, ex-communist, ERC politician Jaume Miravitlles, and CADCI president and representative for the *Partit Català Proletari* (Catalan Proletarian Party) Pere Aznar were appointed as vice-presidents. They were supported by the CCEP, which declared its intent to "declare war on forces destructive to human values and rebut fascism."[12] Trabal quickly announced his intent to serve as a foil to the exclusivist games in Berlin and the class-limited events of the Workers' Olympiads, with *La Vanguardia* later stating "Señor Trabal noted that the games did not have a class or party agenda but aimed to unite the youth of the world under a common goal of progress, liberty and peace."[13]

The choice to meet at the CADCI offices may seem strange, but the union had an established past in the world of popular sport. As early as 1906 the CADCI building had contained a gymnasium with the goal of "facilitating the practice of physical culture necessary for the members to secure the best conditions in life."[14] The CADCI had also established it legitimacy politically after being shut down during Primo de Rivera's dictatorship. Its teams had made notable appearances in virtually every level of Catalan sport during the Republic, and the organization had been a long-time supporter of the ERC, making it a perfect place for government and civil society organizations to come together and plan the events. Many of the union's members would have also been involved in the organization of the games, from securing lodging for athletes with local families to ensuring that stadia and facilities were both available and accessible to travelling and local athletes alike. It was through this kind of logistical support that the games could be organized on such a shoestring budget.

CADCI was not the only civil society group who helped organize and support the games. The venerable AEP had a long-established relationship with sport and inter-nationalism and had even employed a Swiss gymnastics teacher during the dictatorship.[15] The Ateneu movement was based on an ideal of mutually funded popular education and had its roots in the same liberal romanticism which had begun the Catalan cultural renaissance.[16] The AEP was a particularly notable cross-class associative space, featuring a library and offering its members many classes as well as access to sporting and cultural activities and even affordable foodstuffs. The *Partit Comunista Català* (Catalan Communist Party) as well as several anarchist groups had their intellectual and organizational roots in the AEP, which now lent its considerable organizational expertise to the task of supporting the Popular Olympics.

The organizations supporting the games also contributed specific expertise or interests. One such group was the CFE, a progressive feminist organization that was the first women-only sport club in Spain and which aimed to be accessible to all classes of interested women. The club promoted education as well as exercise and was well connected within the intellectual circles of Barcelona. Not only did the CFE publish its own periodical, its leadership also frequently contributed to sports publications such as *La Rambla de Catalunya*[17] to remind readers of the importance of physical culture in creating the modern Catalan woman. It was these modern Catalan women who would have competed in the Popular Olympics had they not instead found themselves fighting alongside their comrades in the Popular Militia.

The overlap in personnel was not the only reason that the Popular Olympics' organizing committee mooched space from a well-established union; there was also a financial imperative. The games, pulled together at such short notice, had a miniscule budget. This was not a hurdle to the organizers who were familiar with poverty wages and vanishingly small budgets. Indeed, the popular character of the games was enhanced by the lack of funds available. Housing, for instance, was something that could be provided by local workers rather than built at great expense. Stadia existed and could be requisitioned for such a necessary event. Travel to the games would likely mean crossing France, and so an appeal was made to the solidarity of French unions.[18] Soon, through their inter-national working-class solidarity network, the COOP had built a pot-luck Olympiad that would challenge the years of planning and millions of marks invested in the Berlin games.

It was not only athletes who came from afar. In a letter to the British Trades Union Congress, the organization stated that it had the "moral and financial" support of both "the Catalonian and Spanish government", but also asked them to provide whatever they could lest this moral support fall short. The British Workers' Sport Association sold commemorative stamps, allegedly by the tens of thousands, in order to fund and grow their team.[19] Meanwhile, in Norway and Paris, games were organized to raise funds to send a team South to Barcelona.[20] Norway, like Spain, had developed a sporting sphere in the inter-war period and was thus able to quickly adapt to new popular sporting ideas as it had a less entrenched sporting civil society. Presumably, the solidarity networks established through the Popular Front by political exiles as well as those forged at the CIREO conference and at Workers' Olympiads combined with a general distaste for the Berlin games on the left funded the majority of this support. Even where financial backing was hard to come by, there was also an opportunity for some groups to give support to the games through their own labour. It was with the cooperation of French transport unions and the newly minted Popular Front government that a free train was provided to ensure entrants could make it to Barcelona in time for the games.[21]

Of course, support was not universal. The Catalan and Spanish right decried the games, associating them with what they saw as the corrupting influence of Jews and communists. *La Publicitat* went as far as to run an article by Pierre de Coubertin himself on July 19.[22] The Baron was no longer at the realm of the IOC and seemed somewhat sympathetic to the Nazi cause, as were many of those who opposed the Popular Olympics.

GOVERNMENT FUNDING

Placing the Catalan nation at the forefront of a progressive and anti-fascist European nationalism was very much part of the ERC's agenda in 1936. Catalan independence had long been opposed by the Spanish right, and the Spanish right had recently been supported by fascist powers in Italy and Germany. Forming inter-national alliances was crucial to the survival of the nation that the ERC was building in Barcelona and that which its Popular Front allies were constructing in Madrid. However, it was not only the Catalan government which supported the games; taxpayers around Europe footed their share of the bill for a games that was inter-national in its character, goals, and funding. It is through the Popular Olympics that we see how the Popular Front envisioned a fraternal, cooperative, and progressive nationalism in which each nation supported the others. These events would show the world the power of a system of alliances that stood opposed to racism and in favour of a healthier, happier, and more inter-national cross-class left. Thus, support for the games came not only from Catalonia, but also from its allies in the Popular Front.

The Popular Olympics were not the first games that Catalonia put on to unite athletes from diverse nations against fascism. In addition to invitational races like the Xallenge República (which celebrated the fifth anniversary of the founding of the Republic),[23] the CCEP also held multisport events before the Popular Olympics. The Copa Thälmann (sometimes also referred to as the Trofeo Thalemann) was named after an executed German communist and held from April 11 to 13, 1936, and was in many ways a precursor to the Popular Olympics. The event united regional teams from across Spain, with officials from as far afield as Hungary, in events that show strong links to those scheduled for the Popular Olympics.[24] The use of Thälmann's name indicated that the CCEP intended to speak to the world with its events. That same name, Thälmann, would return to Barcelona in 1937 over the heads of German volunteers who made up the International Brigade's Thälmann Centuria, which later became a battalion of over 1500 volunteers who came to Spain from German-speaking countries to fight a battle they hoped to one day fight again in their own nations.

The naming of the event, and its intent to encompass "the spirit of anti-fascism,"[25] show that the CCEP was, from its outset, a body intended to place Catalonia at the forefront of a global anti-fascist movement. The event finished just one day before the fifth anniversary of the proclamation of Spain's Second Republic, and teams from across Iberia were welcomed. As was the norm for the popular sports movement, things were pulled together at short notice. Newspapers carried adverts just two weeks before inviting any interested citizens to try out.[26] Despite such short notice, attendance was good, and the spectacle was received positively by fans and the sporting media. Madrid, Castile, Valencia, and Asturias were represented alongside Catalonia. The event gave a nod to the inter-nationalism of the games that were to come with the inclusion of a Hungarian referee. Contests in boxing, athletics, gymnastics, swimming, and wrestling took place in various facilities. Football took centre stage, but the halftime break was filled with a mass relay race that pitted athletes from various sports against each other in regional teams.[27] The goal here was to reward the healthiest and most rounded citizenry, not the elite performance.

FOOTING THE BILL

In order to move from the smaller spectacles of April to the larger events planned in July, the COOP would require significant resources. As an inter-nationally connected and articulated event, the Popular Olympics was never likely to be funded by a single nation, especially a nation without a state. Much of the spending for the games had already been undertaken by the time the COOP was formed. The infrastructure required for a large event was in place thanks to the 1929 Exposition and the Catalan love for building "cathedrals" for sport. The practice of grafting Olympics onto World's Fairs was not a new one; indeed, without it the modern Olympic movement might have fizzled out in its early years. The popular sport organizations which had existed under the ERC since 1931 were ready and willing to lend their energy to the organization and staffing of the games, and they had the support of governments and civil society groups across Europe. The Popular Olympics were hosted by a city and funded by a movement. The Popular Front would pay for the games that would have briefly made Barcelona its capital.

Madrid's Popular Front government allotted 300,000 pesetas to support the games.[28] As well as a financial aid, this was an important symbolic donation. Not only did the economic contribution make the events possible, but it also increased the legitimacy of the events. The support of a state government allowed other governments to support team efforts in Barcelona without fear of offending the government in Madrid by supporting a Catalan separatist event. Madrid's donation reinforced the idea that, during this Third Biennium, Barcelona and Madrid shared a goal of creating a left-Republican unity and opposing fascism and the right within a unified Popular Front. While the games certainly did embrace Catalan nationalism, the support of Madrid shows that what was being promoted was a Catalan nation within a greater popular Spain, and indeed a Popular Front embracing all of Europe.

To this, the Generalitat added 100,000 pesetas of its own, and the city of Barcelona made a monetary donation of an unspecified amount.[29] The COOP remarked that "[e]xtensive support on the part of the City of Barcelona can certainly be counted on" and that the mayor of Barcelona was chiefly concerned with "technical questions."[30] Collectors stamps were issued to fund both the Popular Olympics and the Copa Thälmann, although the exact number issued is unspecified; however, they are still relatively easy to encounter among collectors today.[31] The city itself also shouldered the burden of finding lodging for visiting athletes (which was free) as well as stadia for the games and volunteers for all manner of jobs that needed to be done in order to allow the huge event to come together in just three months. Without the support of the Barcelona City Hall, it would have been hard to imagine the Popular Front summoning the finances to construct or even find stadia in time for a games that would stand against the spectacle in Berlin.

The French government was the newest and richest member of the Popular Front by the summer of 1936, having succeeded in obtaining 386 seats of the 608 available in the May election. Although they elected to allow French athletes to compete in Berlin, Blum's government did donate a significant sum to help the Popular Olympics occur and was not shy about making this publicly known. News of the donation was met with delight in Barcelona, with the COOP issuing a press release stating that

> [w]ith this decision of the French government, with France's official participation in the Peoples' Olympiad at Barcelona, it has become a world event. Today the Peoples' Olympiad at Barcelona is the greatest inter-national sport institution, incorporating the true Olympic spirit. The democratic countries

of Europe have a mission to fulfil: the defense of human freedom, culture and
progress. All adherents of these ideals should miss no opportunity of carrying
out their mission. The Peoples' Olympiad in Barcelona is such an opportunity.
France has set an example to the democratic countries. If only those countries
that call themselves democratic would follow this example.[32]

Clearly the foreign funding was part of the narrative of the organizers,
who intended to showcase the inter-national nature of the games. This
French donation, combined with the positive replies from interested athletes, led the organizers to proclaim that the games were to be extended
by three days on the very same day they announced the donation. Clearly,
things were going better than even the ideologues behind the event could
have imagined a month earlier.

In her recollection of the atmosphere before the games, US-based journalist Muriel Rukeyser notes that "France had asked for more money for
these games than the sum allotted to the big Olympics."[33] A press release
by the COOP in mid-June noted that a donation of half a million francs
from Paris expressed not only the "official" participation of France (the
word was underlined in the document) but also the fact that the Popular
Olympics were "the greatest international sport institution incorporating
the true Olympic spirit."[34] The same document suggests that French newspaper *L'Auto* had reported a cut in the budget of the team attending the
Berlin games to fund this new contingent, although the Berlin games still
received 1 million francs, twice the funding allotted to the Popular Olympics.

On June 29 of that year, the French cabinet announced an increase in
the grant, to 600,000 francs (at the rates of exchange published in *La
Vanguardia*, June 7, 1936, this was about 290,000 pesetas). Even three
weeks before the games, this extra support would have been vital to their
success and allowed the organizers to further support the travel of interested parties. Companys responded to the news with a telegram to Blum,
acknowledging "the brotherly action of the French government in its support of the Barcelona games."[35] It seems that both leaders were willing to
share the funding and prestige of the games, a sharp contrast to IOC
games then and since.

Alongside these monetary donations, France also provided infrastruc-
tural support, such as a special train, which was joined by another train
carrying 500 athletes from Switzerland and then left Paris on July 16 and
carried competitors from France and anyone else wishing to travel to the
games.[36] There was also cooperation on passport processing and special
visas for athletes transiting France on their way to Barcelona. Blum's

government in Paris also designated July 5 as "Peoples' Olympiad Day" to raise funds and awareness. A representative for the COOP would fly to Paris and be met by the French ministers for aviation and sport (Cot and Lagrange, respectively).[37] Paris had supported the concept of the Popular Olympics even before Barcelona had offered to host them; it was at the CIREO conference in Paris that the boycott movement became aware of the Catalan willingness to promote an alternative to the Berlin games. It is not a stretch to say that Paris was as important as Madrid and Barcelona in making the games viable, a true realization of the promise of the Popular Front.

According to Andres Martin, there was also a Swiss monetary contribution which, along with the extra investment from Paris, made the games viable.[38] This may have been the 2000-franc donations from three cantons which is mentioned in earlier correspondence by the COOP[39]; if the 6000 pesetas amount is correct, this would equate to just over 13,600 pesetas at 1936 exchange rates.[40] The support of multiple states made it possible for a games to occur in a way that ensured that all participants were equally invested. Where modern Olympiads measure their legacy in terms of national sports participation and prestige following the spectacle events, the payoff for the Popular Games would be inter-national, just like the funding.

Often it is suggested that the Popular Olympics were a creature of the communist or socialist sporting bodies, but nowhere in the documentary record is there any evidence of this. In early 1936 the RSI wrote to several Workers' Sport bodies, including the FCDO, to ask if they would consider organizing an alternative to the Berlin games. In April, the CCEP responded with a request for funding, but there seems to be no record of a response.[41] In fact, donations came mostly from Popular Front and civil society groups, with no money arriving from explicitly communist governments (although communists were often included in the Popular Front). This was not, in terms of finances, ideology, or participation, an extension of the Workers' Olympic movement or the Spartakaiads. Instead, the Popular Olympics was a unique representation of the Popular Front and its opposition to fascism and the hijacking of the Olympic movement by fascists.

CONCLUSIONS

The combined donation to the COOP did not amount to a huge sum of money, just 700,000 pesetas plus whatever contribution the city of Barcelona and the Swiss made. The Berlin games are estimated to have cost 30 million US dollars, although it is hard to estimate accurately given that most capital spending was shouldered by the government. Certainly 16.5 million marks (1.25 million USD[42]) were spent on decoration alone.[43] The Barcelona games 700,000 pesetas in confirmed donations equate to just over 85,000 US dollars.[44] Obviously, the costs of stadia, infrastructure, and even transport were already met or were funded from other sources, but the extraordinary thrift of an event that showed no signs of failure and succeeded in bringing tens of thousands of athletes and spectators is nothing short of remarkable and illustrates the ingenuity and solidarity of the Popular Front.

Even during the three months that the COOP existed, it was able to demonstrate the value of the cross-class and public-private partnerships that lay at the core of the popular sport model. The Popular Olympics would not have been possible without the support of actors from the state level down to the villages and towns of Catalonia who hosted and supported athletes on their way to the games. The ERC's willingness to fill the hole that was left for many by the absence of a legitimate Olympics in 1936 showed its desire to lead the Popular Front and its conviction that sport could be used as both domestic and foreign policy. The fact that it lacked the resources to support this but went ahead anyway illustrates the faith placed in the emerging solidarity networks that existed between the extremes of fascism and communism and outside the apathy of the major capitalist powers.

In total, at least three states, four nations, and dozens of civil society groups helped to share the tab for the Popular Olympics. There was no money from Moscow or the Comintern. The funding of these games was every bit as unique as the idea behind them. Somewhere between Berlin and Bolshevism, without the funding or apparatus of totalitarian ideology, Barcelona asked everyone who shared its rejection of the manipulation of sport to chip in and support a gathering that would bring together nations and races and cement their solidarity through sweat and shared experience.

NOTES

1. Josep Sauret Pont, "Juegos Olímpicos de Los Trabajadores. Una Visión Artistics Desde Las Vinetas," *Citius, Altius, Fortius* 9, no. 2 (November 1, 2016).
2. David Goldblatt, *The Games: A Global History of the Olympics* (WW Norton & Company, 2018).

3. Andrés Martín, "El Éxito de La Olimpiada Popular Está Asegurado," *Mundo Obrero*, June 29, 1936.
4. Greg Andranovich, "Flipping the City," in *CSSOR 2019 Conference* (CSSOR, Fullerton, Ca, 2009). Ironically, Barcelona's 1992 games would come to be the paramount example of the use of mega events as urban regeneration.
5. COOP. "Press Service. English Edition, No. 7," June 29, 1936.
6. "Esport I Ciutadania." *l'Acció.* July 11, 1936.
7. COOP, "Press Service. English Edition, No. 5," June 1, 1936.
8. The first press reference to it is in April, but this is a reference to it promoting events suggesting it was founded earlier.
9. Mundo Deportivo 18 March 1936 pp6.
10. Balaguer. "El Camp Nou 'esports de La UE Balaguerina." Pla I Muntanya, September 22, 1930.
11. "Esport," *Justicia Social,* May 25, 1936.
12. Note from the CCEP published in *Justicia social* 23 May 1936 pp3 in Pujadas, X., and C. Santaca. "L'altra Olimpiada." Barcelona '36. Barcelona, Llibres de l'Index (1990) pp73.
13. La Vanguardia 17th June, 1936.
14. CADCI, *Seccio Permanent d'Esports i Excursions: Reglament* (CADCI, 1931).
15. The teacher, Emili Pelicier, frequently contributed exercises and advice to the Ateneu's newsletter. See Emili Pelicier, "Gimnasticsa Util i Gimnastica Perjudicial," Butlletí AEP, April 1, 1923.
16. Pere Sola, *Els Ateneus Obrers i La Cultura Popular a Catalunya (1900–1939)* (Barcelona, 1978); Angel Duarte Montserrat, *Possibilistes y Federals: Política y Cultura Republicanes a Reus (1874–1899)*, 1992, http://dialnet.unirioja.es/servlet/libro?codigo=185590; Ramón Flecha, "Spanish Society and Adult Education," *International Journal of Lifelong Education* 9, no. 2 (1990): 99–108, https://doi.org/10.1080/0260137900090203.
17. See, for example, Anna Martinez-Sagi, "Els Drets de La Dona," *La Rambla*, November 23, 1931.
18. "Un Tren Especial Desde París," *El Mundo Deportivo*, July 6, 1936.
19. "Press Information." British Workers' Sport Association, June 24, 1936. Archives of the Trades Union Congress.
20. COOP. "Press Service. English Edition, No. 7," June 29, 1936.
21. "Un Tren Especial Desde París," *El Mundo Deportivo*, July 6, 1936.
22. Pierre de Coubertin, *La Publicitat,* July 19, 1936.
23. "La Volta a Barcelona (Xallenge República): Camí, Gunyador." *La Humanitat,* March 14, 1936.
24. Adria, "El Trofeo Copa Thalemann," *El Mundo Deportivo*, April 13, 1936.
25. Adria, "El Trofeo Copa Thalemann," *El Mundo Deportivo*, April 13, 1936.

26. "Los Festivales Proximos Del Comité Cátala Pro Esport Popular," *Mundo Deportivo*, March 30, 1936.
27. Adria, "El Trofeo Copa Thalemann," *El Mundo Deportivo*, April 13, 1936.
28. *El Mundo Deportivo*, June 18, 1936.
29. J. G. Candau, J. A. Samaranch, and G. P. B. Martínez, *El Deporte En La Guerra Civil* (Espasa, 2007).
    G. Colomé and J. Sureda, "Sport and International Relations (1913–1939): The 1936 Popular Olympiad," *Centre d'Estudis Olímpics UAB*. Http://Olympicstudies.Uab.Es/Pdf/Wp020_eng.Pdf (Accessed March 18, 2008). Gounot suggests that the city contributed the same as the Generalitat, but no footnote is offered for this.
30. COOP, "Press Service. English Edition, No. 5," June 1, 1936.
31. Josep Sauret Pont, "Juegos Olímpicos de Los Trabajadores. Una Visión Artistics Desde Las Vinetas," *Citius, Altius, Fortius* 9, no. 2 (November 1, 2016).
32. COOP, "Press Service. English Edition, No. 6," June 18, 1936.
33. Muriel Rukeyser. "We Came for Games." *Esquire*, October 1, 1974.
34. "Press Service. English Edition, No. 6," June 18, 1936. Archives of the Trades Union Congress.
35. COOP. "Press Service. English Edition, No. 7," June 29, 1936.
36. "Un Tren Especial Desde París," *El Mundo Deportivo*, July 6, 1936.
37. COOP. "Press Service. English Edition, No. 7," June 29, 1936.
38. Andrés Martín, "El Éxito de La Olimpiada Popular Está Asegurado," *Mundo Obrero*, June 29, 1936.
39. COOP, "Press Service. English Edition, No. 6," June 18, 1936.
40. "Foreign Exchange Rates 1913–1941 #7: Switzerland's Independence; Turkey Avoids Devaluation," New World Economics, accessed October 24, 2018, https://newworldeconomics.com/foreign-exchange-rates-1913-1941-7-switzerlands-independence-turkey-avoids-devaluation/.
41. A Gounot. "El Proyecto de La Olimpiada Popular de Barcelona (1936), Entre Comunismo Internacional y Republicanismo Regional." *Cultura, Ciencia y Deporte*, no. 3 (2005): 115.
42. Harold Marcuse, "Historical Dollar-to-Marks Currency Conversion Page," accessed October 3, 2018, http://www.history.ucsb.edu/faculty/marcuse/projects/currency.htm#tables.
43. Frank Zarnowski, "A Look at Olympic Costs" (Mount St. Mary's College), accessed October 3, 2018, http://library.la84.org/SportsLibrary/JOH/JOHvlnl/JOHvlnlf.pdf.
44. http://eh.net/hmit/exchangerates/.

CHAPTER 4

The Participants

Abstract This chapter looks in detail at the promised delegations who were in Barcelona or on their way there when the Civil War began. Through press releases, newspaper articles, and other archival documents, it attempts to profile many of the individuals who would have competed at Barcelona and illustrates the journey that took athletes to Barcelona. It also deals with the differences between popular and Workers' Sport in order to address the misconception that the Popular Olympics were part of the socialist sport movement.

Keywords Popular Olympics • Workers' Sport • Anti-fascism • Spanish Second Republic

On August 11, 2012, Mo Farrah, a Somali-born British athlete, won the 5000-m gold medal to cheers that shook the stadium to such an extent that the photo finish camera was rendered unable to capture a clear image. Athletes make the headlines at the Olympics, but beneath the individuals is an equally important narrative of nation, inclusion, and belonging. These narratives are not always carried over into everyday life, as Britain so amply demonstrated, but they can provide valuable stepping stones to help solidify and create identities. Even if just for a moment, there was a moment when even the most unreconstructed colonialists joined the whole of Britain in cheering for a Muslim man who had put off his Ramadan fast to make his adopted homeland proud.

In 1936, there were many athletes who found themselves without a homeland. The rise of the right had pushed Jews, communists, LGBTQ people, and Romany people out of Germany and the surrounding nations as Nazi influence grew. Italian exiles also flooded France and Spain. Meanwhile in the USA, people of colour and those on the left often faced incarceration for advocating for an inclusion of their beliefs in a con-strained political system. Even in Spain itself, two nations existed, and each could not see a future in which the other was allowed to survive. This fractured politics would ultimately lead to a global conflict, but in 1936 it caused a global dislocation which bought people together and allowed for new and different inter-national identities to emerge.

IDEOLOGY

In this climate of fracture, the Popular Olympics offered a unity that was based on shared principles, tolerance, and an acceptance of diversity. Their goal was "the uniting of all antifascist sportsmen from whatever camp they may come."[1] The philosophy behind the Popular Olympics seems to have been rooted in a belief that playing together and agreeing on basic prin-ciples of non-discrimination and equality could bring the people of the world closer and an ideology could grow out of this experience rather than be reinforced by it.

The Berlin boycott movement had momentarily united a very diverse range of people opposed to fascism. This offered the perfect moment for Catalonia to leap onto the world stage and offer a sporting platform for the demonstration of political unity. The Popular Olympics would be a welcoming place for anyone who wished to oppose what they saw coming in Berlin; they would bring together "[e]veryone who is against fascism, this modern plague, who [sic] is against systems based on force, that per-secute beliefs, races and opinions" and "not a means of putting over pro-paganda for one country or one party under the cloak of athletic games."[2] This ideology goes not just for the Popular Olympics but also for the Popular Front.

"It is necessary to give a practical demonstration of the international anti-fascist sport, and it is just this that the People's Olympiad is going to do,"[3] proclaimed the organizing committee of the games a month before they were due to begin. The Catalans did not know just how quickly war would be a reality for them, but the conflicts of 1934 made it clear that the Spanish right was not willing to cede power without spilling blood. Therefore, these games served not just to create unity, but to demonstrate the power that lay behind that unity. The Popular Olympics would give anti-fascism a meaning and an image beyond that of the speeches and articles which had characterized much of the formation of the Popular Front. The discord and uproar around the Berlin Olympics presented an opportunity that allowed the Popular Front speak to what it stood for as well as what it stood against.

PROMOTION

In order for these games to genuinely represent an anti-fascist global Popular Front, it needed to pull athletes from across Europe and the other side of the Atlantic. The organizers promised that this would indeed be a place where nations and races came together on the "giant oval" of the Montjuïc stadium. Men and women, black and white, Jew, Muslim, and atheist, would compete at the games in a pointed affront to the events in Berlin. Organizers were very clear that "fascists have no place [in these games] having shown themselves to be enemies of popular culture;"[4] however, all others were welcome.

The challenge facing the organizers was how to best get out the word about their event. Given that the entire operation was conceptualized, organized, and publicized within 11 weeks and that this was the age of the telegram, not the tweet, that was no small challenge. It was for this reason that the games chiefly relied upon the familiar networks of the left. These networks of unions, socialist parties, and their associated sports organizations were long established and reliable but did not extend to the new groups who had been allied to the Popular Front in recent months. It was these groups that distinguished the Popular Olympics from Workers' Sport, and it was their participation that the organizers flaunted, even in their communications with unions and Workers' Sport bodies.

The one tendency in inter-national sport which was close in ideology to that of the Popular Olympics was the Workers' Sport movement. Many historians have suggested that the Workers' Sport and Popular Olympics were one and the same, but doing so misses the unique value and timing of the Popular Olympics. Certainly, the two movements shared the left wing of the political spectrum and even a few participants, but the Popular Olympics were not an avatar of the more ideologically constrained Workers' Sport movement. It is true that the Popular Olympics encompassed

Workers' Sport, but they also appealed to a broader constituency, much in the same way that the Popular Front encompassed the socialist parties of Europe but also a wider range of social democrats and bourgeois liberals.

Workers' Sports were explicitly class-based and designed to promote inter-national proletarian unity. Certainly, this was not a choice that was made exclusively by the workers; bourgeois sporting institutions, including the IOC, had long used amateurism codes to ensure that only people of the appropriate class had enough leisure time to compete in the Olympics. These codes meant that fencing coaches could compete, as they were considered members of polite society, but any athlete who relied on exhibition races or sponsors for things as minor as travel funding or entry fees might see themselves ruled as ineligible.[5] Workers were largely unable to devote the time and income to their sporting practice that the bourgeois could, excluding them from IOC sports with strict amateur codes. In response to this, and in order to strengthen global working-class solidarity, the Workers' Sports movement emerged.

Workers' Sport events may not have been as well-celebrated in the historical record as the IOC's games, but they often dwarfed the early gatherings of the IOC and its affiliated governing bodies. Kidd has called the movement "explicitly class conscious, partly by the design of the trade unions and political parties which sponsored it and partly by circumstance."[6] Workers' Olympiads, the creation of the Socialist Workers' Sport International (SWSI), and Spartakiads put on by the Moscow-backed Red Sports International (RSI) often included spectacles designed to illustrate and reinforce the importance of class struggle. So specific were these games in their ideology that they, along with most of the European left, split into two factions and each refused to play with the other.

In many nations across Europe, it was in Workers' Sports that better performances and tougher competition could be found.[7] Working-class athletes didn't lack talent, but they often lacked the means, time, or the status to join the elite clubs and universities which were represented at the IOC's Olympics. Workers' Sport rejected the commercialization of sport and often stood against the spending of state funds on spectator stadia as opposed to facilities for mass participation sports. In the 1920s, the spectacles at Workers' events were not limited to sports performances; they included mock battles between the "world proletariat" and the "world bourgeoisie"[8] and the collapsing of a symbolic tower that represented global capitalism.[9] Clearly the message was one of unity against a foe, but the foe was capitalism, not fascism.

The Popular Olympics, in the spirit of the Popular Front, did away with this rhetoric of class war and instead aimed to welcome social democrats and liberals so long as they were prepared to reject fascism. The Popular Olympics were about demonstrating and celebrating unity rather than expressing anger or opposition. Catalan and Spanish affiliates of the Workers' Sport inter-nationals made it clear that they were only part of the organizational coalition behind the Popular Olympics, not all of it. Andres Martin, head of Spain's Worker's Sport body the FCDO, stated in an article at the time that anyone suggesting the Popular Olympics were a "red" games was "knowingly lying."[10] His assertion seems to be confirmed by the shift in symbolism. The singing and dancing spectacles hosted at the popular games would be more focused on collaboration than conflict, and there would be no collapsing of symbolic towers here (there were plans to engage in the age-old Catalan tradition of building human towers or *Castells*). Although there was clearly a common enemy, the focus here was on building an alternative global future, not on simply opposing a backwards European ideology.

The Popular Olympics were an outgrowth of the ERC's popular sports movement which had great success with using mass participation sports to bring the various classes of the Catalan nation who made up its electoral coalition onto the same playing field. This model had made progress in breaking down the class divisions that caused the Workers'/elite sport dichotomy. The Workers' Sport movement aimed to unite one class across the world; the popular sport movement aimed to unite classes through sport. As the Popular Olympics' propaganda noted, these games were "the climax of the new Spanish peoples' sport"[11] and not part of the distinct European Workers' Sport tradition.

However, an Olympiad would be a sad affair without athletes, and the Workers' Sport federations were the obvious place to look. Their athletes would be excluded from the Berlin games on grounds of ideology, professionalism, cost, and, in many cases, personal safety. It was to their colleagues on the left that the COOP appealed when the time came to invite athletes to the Olympics. The CIREO, held earlier in 1936, was largely attended by those at the forefront of the boycott movement. It was likely through contacts that were cemented here that the COOP reached out to organize their own event. Many of those attending would have been from the traditional leftist organizations, and one assumes that Workers' Sport bodies would have been well represented, but this was not an official Workers' Sport event. Left-wing sports groups were joined by Jewish and other anti-Nazi groups, just as they would be in Barcelona a few months later.

A press release in June 1936 made clear that "all athletes without exception, to whatever association they belong, may participate in the Popular Olympics at Barcelona" before mentioning that, due to its exclusion from the Berlin games, the FSGT would be heavily represented in Barcelona.[12] Obviously the FSGT, which united France's Workers' Sport bodies, had been present at the conference. Meanwhile, communications in the UK were addressed not directly to the Workers' Sport body, but to the Trades Union Congress (TUC), the body which had attended the same conference for the UK.[13] Likewise, letters were sent to Swiss and US-based Workers' Sport organization, but in these letters, it was stressed that this Olympiad would appeal to a broader constituency than those of the SWSI or RSI and that these organizations must share the burden of broadening the reach and appeal of alternatives to the IOC games.[14]

It seems that the COOP met with some success. It became necessary to extend the date range of the games from the initially planned four days to a full week, and this extension was made possible by a generous grant from Paris.[15] Seemingly, this high level of attendance came as a shock to the COOP; stamps and posters had been printed and second runs were issued with the new dates as the games grew.[16] Attendance was expected from groups concerned with the rampant anti-Semitism in Germany and racism in the USA as well as those who had been committed to sport as a means of disseminating ideology for some time. In promoting the games, the COOP sent out material suggesting that, "of particular interest to anti-fascists are the Jewish sportsmen coming from Palestine. The teams of exiled German-Jews from Paris and Amsterdam and the Negro sportsmen from the USA."[17] These groups were not the traditional adherents to Workers' Sport and indicated the desire of the COOP and the Popular Olympics to welcome a broader constituency of athletes and anti-fascists to Barcelona.

GENDER

Gender diversity was to be embraced by the COOP, unlike the IOC which had seen De Coubertin resign his position over this and other issues. "The picture of the Peoples' Olympiad would not be complete if woman did not take her due place in it. Particularly in Spain is woman far from being free. That sport, and above all sport of a general, popular character, is one of the best and most important means of achieving women's freedom, cannot be open to doubt... The participation of many women in the Peoples' Olympiad is therefore one of the most important objects which this great institution has to fulfil." However, the low turnout among both domestic and foreign women was troubling to organizers, including the woman who wrote their foreign language press releases.[18] "The foreign delegations, according to the entries to hand, are also dominated by the masculine element, for the most part. Here also the committee will see to it that the foreign women are given prominence," proclaimed the organizing committee. In order to increase the number of women participating, the organizing committee of the games removed all qualification conditions for women's participation.[19]

A more equal participation of women had long been one of the goals of popular sport. From columns focused on women's sport in newspapers[20] to the inclusion of women's clubs in the CCEP and the COOP, the Catalan movement demonstrated a genuine commitment to a more gender-equal sporting landscape. Catalan civil society supported the movement for gender equality, even in organizations that were not specifically "about" gender such as the *Club Natació Barcelona* (CNB), where the coach was Josefina Torrens.[21] In 1934, FC Barcelona changed its constitution to include the word "members" without a specific gender, and not only added a women's team, but also a woman to its board of directors.[22]

Spanish gender ideology had long rested on the Church's imposition of social standards and a concept of "differential endocrinology" which held women as physically incapable of equality. Medical doctor Gregorio Marañón's work entitled "Sexo, trabajo y deporte" provides an example of the prevailing attitude. Marañón was a Republican and a professor of endocrinology at the Compultense in Madrid from 1931. In his essays, he argued that the female body was ill-suited to adapting to public sphere life and the physical demands of sport. The essays provided "evidence" in the form of a table asserting male and female physical and emotional traits. His major thesis seems to have been that the female body was designed to raise children and was ill-equipped emotionally or physically for life outside of the home. He even asserted that women's muscles and bones were weaker than those of men and that their "primary sexual characteristics" were maternity, child raising, and domestic work, whereas men were predisposed to "defending and providing for the family." Such theories, and their acceptance, served as an impediment to change in gender roles, especially in physical culture.[23]

Catalan feminists had long seen feminism as a social movement, and about much more than juridical rights. Just as the Catalan nation had made use of physical culture to move from rhetoric to reality, so did Catalan feminists. The claims of differential endocrinology and female incapability were harder to sustain once men and women had run, jumped, and played together. Given this commitment to experience and not just excellence, great effort was made to ensure that the athletes of the Popular Olympics had a wide range of abilities. The records set at the stadium in Montjuïc would serve as "a means of propaganda for a better hygienic and physical training for the peoples." All competitors would not strive "for tenths of seconds and the glory of victory for their nations" but rather promote the idea of "free popular sport."[24] Again, this was a crucial element of popular sport, which aimed to create healthy communities more than record performances.

Numbers and Nations

The basic agreement on politics that united the Popular Front allowed for nations to define themselves within this "big tent." This meant that, alongside the flags of the states that would have marched into the opening ceremony, there were also nations represented outside of the state structure. Catalonia, the Basque Country, Asturias, Andalucía, and Galicia all sent their own national teams. Morocco, long occupied by Spain and France and often the victim of colonial violence, would compete alone, and not under the flag of its colonizers. Alongside the Moroccans would be Algerians, also competing as their own nation. Exiled victims of fascism would compete, either in the nations where they had found asylum or as teams such as the Hamburg Workers' Turnen Society or Jewish associations in Paris or Antwerp. These teams were not designed to enforce the concept of national competition, so much as inter-national solidarity.

A variety of differing identities were possible when the barriers between nation states were reduced and all were united under a common banner such as that of the Popular Front. Indeed, Article 30 of the Olympic Charter requires only that a nation be "an independent State recognized by the international community" in order to qualify for Olympic representation.[25] This threshold is somewhat lower than that required for admission to many other inter-national bodies, and although this law remained largely uninvoked to problematize colonial identities, it was present from the outset of the modern Olympic movement. In Catalonia, the difference between nation and state was obvious, and this must have contributed to the decision to allow representation of any national community that imagined itself as bound through space and time rather than merely state entities with a government and a military. Colonized people and exiled people would have marched into the stadium on the 19th of July with equal status to those who had the full support of their governments.

In a letter sent at the end of June 1936, the COOP claimed that the representatives of each nation planning to attend were numerous:

> France, 1500. England 50. Holland 20. Norway 30. Denmark (only Chess up to the present) 3. Belgium 60. Sweden 30. Soviet Union (number yet unknown but a strong delegation is at any rate to be expected). Switzerland 250. Czechoslovakia 50. Austria (whose sportsmen have no opportunity of public participation) 4. Palestine 30. Algiers 120. Hungarian (Paris emigration) 30. Jewish Associations (Paris, Antwerp, etc....) about 150. USA (for which travelling expenses are particularly high) 8. Morocco 50. Germany (emigration) 18.

Teams from Ireland and Portugal were also expected. In total, 2000 foreign athletes and 8000 from Spain and Catalonia were expected. In addition, special trains from Geneva and Asturias would bring 500 fans each, trains from Paris would carry fans and athletes for free, and a ship from England was expected with a similar number of spectators.[26]

France provided by far the largest delegation from outside of Iberia. As fellow members of the Popular Front, this event signalled not just a chance to reclaim the Olympic legacy but an opportunity to reinforce ties between the ideologically aligned governments in Paris, Madrid, and Barcelona. The FSGT conducted trials in the months leading up to the event. Such was the demand that not all interested athletes could attend the Popular Olympics and so a selection had to be made. Although the Workers' Sports organization provided the infrastructure and officials, these trials welcomed all interested athletes in the spirit of the Popular Front. In addition to Workers' Sports affiliates, the games also welcomed the French official rugby team and athletes affiliated to the International Walking Federation. On July 5, Paris hosted a "Popular Olympics Day" to increase awareness and raise funds. Thanks to this broad appeal and effective publicity effort, the French delegation included 1000 members of the FSGT and 500 of other organizations[27] (many more than the 215 athletes from the same nation sent to Berlin[28]).

Alongside the nominally French team, independent teams also came from the province of Alsace and the city of Algiers (probably a reference to all of Algeria). The World Committee of the Student Movement for Peace and Freedom would also send a team from its Paris headquarters.[29] The French government's support of an event which recognized the national status of both colonized people and provinces with a distinct identity within France shows their commitment to the Popular Front and its idea of a supernational identity that would allow for the development of various national identities beneath a broad umbrella.

The Swiss team included "a complete army of first aid workers,"[30] League of Nations observers based in Lausanne, and university professors to aid with the hosting of the games. Pujadas and Santancana state that 200 Swiss athletes were planning to take part in the games.[31] This diverse contingent would represent a nation with an established Workers' Sport tradition. A debate had even taken place in the Swiss Parliament about funding their delegation to Barcelona and withdrawing donations to those on their way to Berlin. A delegate from the SATUS (*Schweizerischer Arbeiter- Turn- und Sportverband*, Swiss Workers' Sports Federation) also noted, "We are in agreement with everything that the popularization of sport represents." The Swiss had long supported the ERC, donating them space at the Swiss-hosted European Congress of nations in 1934. The Swiss would send a range of athletes, as well as several football teams of various levels to the games alongside their logistical support staff. Zurich, Basel, and Geneva branches of SATUS each contributed 2000 Swiss francs towards sending teams, and a special train was to be scheduled to ensure the safe and prompt arrival of the team.[32]

Belgian teams, many of whom were part of the organizations which would help support the 1937 Workers' Olympics in Antwerp, would likely travel through France on the special trains provided by the Popular Front government. Although much closer to Berlin, their choice to side with Barcelona would surely seem wise given the invasion of their small country that was to commence a few years later. The Dutch team were travelling much the same route, and their squad included a woman named Schumann who was said to have refused to participate in the Berlin games despite her medal prospects and elected to go to Barcelona instead.[33] Norwegian participation was also noted. The COOP stated that enthusiasm was high and that the Norwegians were hosting their own national games in June in order to raise funds for their team to travel to Barcelona in July.[34]

Given the pronounced anti-Semitic rhetoric across Europe, there was an unsurprisingly strong presence of Jewish people in the boycott campaign and at the popular games. Leon Blum, a Jewish socialist, was singled out for discrimination by even the Catalan—*La Veu de Catalunya* declared that Blum was "not too French-looking to us."[35] However, this tendency to discrimination was not present in the rhetoric surrounding the games or the Catalan left. Not only were the persecuted Jews welcome in Barcelona, their presence was widely touted to give the event an appeal beyond that of Workers' Sport.

Indeed, the ERC and the COOP welcomed the Jewish exiles to Barcelona so warmly that some chose to remain and fight to defend the Republic. Catalan organizers reached out to the International Zionist Organization and were even able to fund some of the Jewish athletes' travel expenses.[36] It was a half Jewish-German composer, Hans Eisler, who wrote the games' anthem, and the chair of the COOP, Josep Antoni Trabal, had taken part in protests against mistreatment of Jewish people in Germany in the months before the games.[37] There were several thousand Jewish exiles living in Barcelona by the time of the games, and both Jewish and anti-Semitic publications attempted to credit Jews with the organization of the Popular Olympics. In addition to these exiles, athletes from the *Yiddiseher Arbeter Sport Klub* (YASK) in Paris had travelled to the games.[38]

This strong and visible commitment to opposing Nazi anti-Semitism through sport reinforces the idea that these games were more than a gathering of the European left. The Popular Olympics aimed to forge unity between groups opposed to fascism, and to do this, they would need to include one of the most harshly and openly afflicted groups. Indeed, the organizers' best hopes of securing top-level athletes who would have been medal contenders in Berlin may have been Jewish competitors who surely had little choice in not attending the Nazi games.

The Palestinian delegation came from the ranks of Hapoel, a Workers' Sport association who rejected the bourgeois Maccabiah Games that were open only to Jews and the fascist Olympics in Berlin that were essentially closed to Jews, but enthusiastically embraced the Popular Olympics.[39] The Hapoel Palestine football team was one of the most respected competitors in the event, having recently drawn with an elite Hungarian side. The Palestinian team also included Olympic medal contenders in the form of throwing athlete Sonja Lewin-Szmukler, who had come second to Olympic Champion Lilian Copeland in a recent contest, and Los Angeles bronze medalist in wrestling Mickey Hirschl. Hapoel would compete in Barcelona alongside provincial teams of Jewish exiles from Antwerp and Paris who would serve not to set records, but to set the tone of a games which existed in opposition to all that Nazi Germany was doing to Jewish and other people who were not included in its racial vision of the German future.[40]

The Jews were not the only excluded group in Germany. Communists too found themselves murdered, imprisoned, and exiled. Germany had previously hosted one of the strongest Workers' Sport movements in the world, but this movement had not survived the Nazi seizure of power, and the German representation at the Popular Olympics was indicative of the diffusion of the German left. Hamburg was represented by the Workers' Turnen Society. Remnants of the German left were scattered around sympathetic nations, and some of them found their way to Barcelona, where they reunited with their countrymen. Journalist Muriel Rukeyser met "a German who has come to run in the games, on his own, from France where he was working."[41] Clara Thalmann, a Swiss German swimmer representing the *Arbeiterschwimmclubs* (workers' swimming clubs), had a similar story.[42] COOP publications confirm that German exiles in Prague sent a team to the football contest.[43]

Alongside these Germans, a small team of four "free sportsmen" from Austria, which had hosted the previous Workers' Olympics in 1931, arrived a month early for the games and spent their time visiting Lluís Companys and taking a cycling tour of Spain.[44] Hungary, another polity drifting to the right, also sent a team to play water polo (or "waterball" as it is translated in the COOP documents) as well as football, basketball, and athletics and had previously committed officials to the CCEP's Copa Thalemann.[45]

Muriel Rukeyser noted that the people she met after she crossed the border from France were "not Spaniards; they are Catalans. Their own nation, their own language."[46] It was these Catalans that would compete as a nation apart from Spain who would make up the largest team. Catalonia was represented at every level, from elite to provincial. At the highest end of the sporting ladder, FC Barcelona would help in the selection of the elite football team, and local neighbourhood clubs would line up in the third-tier events. The Catalans would be joined by Basques, Andalusians, Galicians, over 500 Asturians,[47] as well as teams from the rest of Spain. These teams had met before, at the Copa Thalemann, and would be even more numerous at the Popular Olympics, where more events were offered and more funds were available. Alongside those nations, the COOP proclaimed that "hardly a university throughout all Spain is to be without entrants."[48] As well as those who came as groups, there were the individual athletes who had decided on boycotting the Olympics in Berlin. The organizers noted that "[t]he Spanish Walking Champion, Roman Castelltort has refused to go to Berlin, even though his club had agreed to meet all his expenses."[49] Between these various constituencies, the Iberian contingent was larger than all the others combined, but also represented several distinct nations within a larger popular Spain.

Rukeyser, who found herself stuck on a train in Montcada when the coup that started the war and stopped the games occurred, quickly found the other attendees from the USA. The US delegation was supported by the "Labor Chest for the Relief and Liberation of Workers of Europe." This delegation, which travelled via London, consisted of two administrators and eight athletes, one of whom was a woman and many of whom planned to compete in several events.[50] The delegation was all based on the East Coast of the USA, where industrial unions had more footing. However, the American Federation of Labor in San Francisco added its support to the "victims of Fascism" and "brave heroes of labor" taking part in the games.[51] A later telegram suggested that more athletes had been added, making the total 12,[52] "with half of them being negroes,"[53] a much better representation ratio than the 18 black men out of 359 US competitors in Berlin. Later, many black volunteers would make the same journey to Spain to defend the Republic. In the war, they would be treated as equals and many served as officers before returning to a USA where they could neither serve nor eat alongside their white comrades.

Also sailing across the Atlantic was the Canadian team. Their representation was small at just six members, but the Canadian athletes were of exceptional quality. Eva Dawes was a high jumper who had world-class potential, having won a bronze medal in the 1932 Los Angeles games. She then followed this feat with a silver in the 1934 British Empire games and a trip to compete in the Soviet Union in 1935. It was this trip that was to end her career; she was suspended for her actions and elected to retire, taking with her Canada's best medal prospects at the 1936 games.

Bruce Kidd's excellent article on the subject outlines the biographies and motivations of this small group of Canadian would-be Olympians. Dawes came out of retirement to compete in Barcelona and clearly had something of an ideological commitment to the cause of the Popular Front. She was joined by two boxers, Norman "Baby" Yack and Sammy Luftspring. Luftspring was proud of his Jewish religion and competed with a Star of David on his shorts. He elected not to put himself forward to compete in Berlin as his parents feared for his life. He professed to being distinctly apolitical, but his desire to travel to Europe and to compete led to him agreeing to Barcelona and persuading his friend Yack, who was also Jewish, to join him. Tom Ritchie and Bill Christie were both sprinters who feared their fitness was not up to the standards required to compete in Berlin; they elected to compete at Barcelona rather than stay at home. Harry Sniderman, who would manage the team, was a whisky salesman who caught wind of the two Jewish boxers and managed to convince the Canadian Jewish Congress to not only support them, but to put on a leaving parade: He achieved this feat in less than 24 hours, showing the kind of acumen that would surely be of great use to a team competing in an Olympiad organized in a matter of weeks.

Thanks to Sniderman's persuasive capacities and despite a record heat wave, over 500 people marched the athletes to their boat which sailed from Montreal for Paris. They would have been a strong team. Luftspring had beaten the boxer who was to be sent to Berlin earlier that year and Dawes had cleared 5'3" in training, which would have seen her win gold in Berlin. Both Christie and Richie had beaten Canadians who won medals in Berlin; their natural speed might have been dulled by the multiple heats in Berlin which would have taxed their lack of form, but they could have prospered in Barcelona.[54]

The Canadians were not alone in the Commonwealth. Britain had its own Popular Front politics and many interested unions and political groups who had formed an active campaign to boycott Berlin and had supported the Popular Olympics from the outset. On June 12, 1936, the COOP sent a formal letter to the British Trades Union Congress inviting them to promote and participate in the coming games which would promote "the true spirit of the Olympiad—The fraternity of peoples and races—Which cannot exist in the atmosphere in Berlin." This letter was also sent to the British Workers' Sport Association and the British Committee for Fair Play in Sport. There was a grant offered to help with the process of transporting athletes across Europe, given that funding had not been secured from Paris yet; this offer might have been based more on hope than on hard cash, but that hope turned out to be justified.

The Paris conference on Fair Play was attended by representatives from the British Workers' Sport Association and TUC who returned to host a national conference at the Trade Union Club in London. This conference, which aimed to "prevent injury to the Olympic Ideals," raised the idea of British athletes attending "a popular sports festival which does not hope for record feats, but does intend to preserve the Olympic spirit." The presence of "Jews and negroes for whom the manifestation of the Olympic Spirit at Barcelona has particular importance" in Barcelona was noted and appreciated by the British supporters of the Popular Olympics who used it to recruit athletes.[55]

The British team, according to communications from the British Workers' Sport Association, was to include "many well-known sportsmen." There were to be 50 athletes in all, and they would travel to the games via a 57-hour train journey. Britain formed a "Committee for the People's Olympiad" under Mr. A. Werner to convene a diverse group of athletes including those from non-IOC sports such as tennis and rugby (the latter having been dropped from the IOC programme in 1924).[56] Notable was the high Welsh representation. Perhaps these athletes were sympathetic to the cause of the Catalan nation, themselves a national minority in a larger state, or perhaps this is merely a reflection of the high union affiliation in industrial Wales.[57] British unions and political organizations of British Jews had been forced together by assault from the right, but the Popular Olympics gave them a chance to showcase the strength with which they could repudiate such attacks.

Perhaps the most intriguing absence at the Barcelona games was that of the USSR. Pre-games reports touted a contingent of 100 athletes from the USSR. At the time Soviet athletes boycotted the IOC's games, and this would have been the largest delegation of Soviet athletes ever to appear in Western Europe.[58] They were confirmed in the football contest, and a breast stroke swimmer named Bersiov who claimed to be the holder of a world record was also promised. However, they did not attend. The ERC, according to COOP Vice President Jaume Miravitlles, was extremely concerned not to portray the games as an extension of the Spartakiad movement.[59] Moscow had begun, in 1935, to rebuild links to international sport. Perhaps its decision to avoid the Barcelona games came out of a fear of offending the IOC and spending even longer as a pariah excluded from the Olympic Games, perhaps they did not wish to see the Popular Olympics dominated by their presence, or perhaps the logistics simply became too complicated. Whatever the reason, the USSR was not represented in the Hotel Olympic on the night of July 18, 1936.

CONCLUSIONS

Orwell reflected on his experience as a foreigner in the Spanish Civil War positively, remarking, "I would sooner be a foreigner in Spain than in most countries. How easy it is to make friends in Spain!" Had it not been for the war that caused Orwell to travel south, one presumes that the athletes at the Popular Olympics would have enjoyed the same experience more peacefully, but doubtless recounted it less eloquently. The Popular Olympics promised to unite a more diverse group of classes and ideologies that would have ever met at the IOC's games or those of the various left-aligned Workers' Sports events. That so many athletes committed to over-looking personal gain and professional advancement in Berlin to instead travel to a games in Barcelona that represented something of an unknown quantity is testament to the organizing capacity of the ERC and the potential strength of the Popular Front. That these athletes would never be able to compete and enact the powerful solidarity on which the games were built is testament to the equally strong ambivalence of the bourgeois democracies and their governments.

NOTES

1. COOP. "Press Service. English Edition, No. 5," June 1, 1936.
2. COOP. "Press Service. English Edition, No. 7," June 29, 1936.
3. COOP. "Letter to Sir Walter Citrine, Secretary, Trades Union Congress General Council," June 18, 1936. Archives of the Trades Union Congress.
4. Mundo Obrero, June 29, 1936.
5. For more on amateurism, see Richard Gruneau, "'Amateurism' as a Sociological Problem: Some Reflections Inspired by Eric Dunning," *Sport in Society* 9, no. 4 (October 1, 2006): 559–82.
6. B. Kidd, "The Popular Front and the 1936 Olympics," *Canadian Journal of the History of Sport and Physical Education* 11, no. 1 (1980): 1–18.
7. For instance, in France, the FSGT Workers' Sport organization saw faster times at its annual championships than were posted at Olympic trials in 1936. Kidd, B. "The Popular Front and the 1936 Olympics." *Canadian Journal of the History of Sport and Physical Education* 11, no. 1 (1980): 1–18.
8. Arnaud, Pierre, and James Riordan. *Sport and International Politics.* London; New York: E & FN Spon, 1998.
9. David Goldblatt. *The Games: A Global History of the Olympics.* London, 2016.
10. Andrés Martín, *Mundo Obrero*, June 29, 1936.
11. "Press Service. English Edition, No. 6," June 18, 1936. Archives of the Trades Union Congress.
12. "Press Service. English Edition, No. 6," June 18, 1936. Archives of the Trades Union Congress.
13. COOP. "Letter to Sir Walter Citrine, Secretary, Trades Union Congress General Council," June 18, 1936. Archives of the Trades Union Congress.

14. COOP. "Press Service. English Edition, No. 6," June 18, 1936.
15. COOP. "Press Service. English Edition, No. 6," June 18, 1936.
16. Josep Sauret Pont, "Juegos Olímpicos de Los Trabajadores. Una Visión Artistics Desde Las Vinetas," *Citius, Altius, Fortius* 9, no. 2 (November 1, 2016).
17. COOP. "Letter to Sir Walter Citrine, Secretary, Trades Union Congress General Council," June 18, 1936. Archives of the Trades Union Congress.
18. Sylvia Martin, *Ink in Her Veins: The Troubled Life of Aileen Palmer* (Apollo Books, 2016).
19. COOP. "Press Service. English Edition, No. 6," June 18, 1936.
20. (Anna Murià) Romaní, "Una Pregunta i Moltes Respostes – Què És l'esport?," *La Rambla*, April 30, 1934. This regular column was written under a pseudonym, but addressed many issues of Women's Popular Sport.
21. Neus Real Mercadal, *El club femení i d'esports de Barcelona, plataforma d'acció cultural* (L'Abadia de Montserrat, 1998).
22. J. Batista, J. M. Bosch, R., Folguera, M., Garí, J., Guardiola, and ... Trabal J. A, "L'obra d'Educació Fisica Popular," *La Veu de Catalunya*, April 3, 1930.
23. Marañón, Gregorio. *Sexo, Trabajo Y Deporte*, 1926.
24. COOP. "Press Service. English Edition, No. 7," June 29, 1936.
25. IOC, "The Olympic Charter" (International Olympic Committee), accessed February 14, 2019, https://stillmed.olympic.org/Documents/olympic_charter_en.pdf.
26. COOP. "Press Service. English Edition, No. 7," June 29, 1936.
27. *Mundo Deportivo*, July 6, 1936.
28. W. J. Murray, "France, Coubertin and the Nazi Olympics: The Response," *Olympika: The International Journal of Olympic Studies* 1 (1992): 46–69.
29. COOP. "Press Service. English Edition, No. 7," June 29, 1936.
30. COOP. "Press Service. English Edition, No. 6," June 18, 1936.
31. X. Pujadas and C. Santacana, "The Popular Olympic Games, Barcelona 1936: Olympians and Antifascists," *International Review for the Sociology of Sport* 27, no. 2 (1992).
32. *Mundo Deportivo*, July 6, 1936.
33. COOP. "Press Service. English Edition, No. 6," June 18, 1936. Archives of the Trades Union Congress.
34. COOP. "Press Service. English Edition, No. 7," June 25, 1936.
35. *La Veu de Catalunya*, July 2, 1936.
36. COOP. "Press Service. English Edition, No. 6," June 18, 1936. Archives of the Trades Union Congress.
37. Raanan Rein, "El Desafio a Los Juegos Olimpicos de Berlin 1936: Los Atleteas Judios de Palestina En La Frustrada Olimpiada Popular de Barcelona," *Historia Contemporánea* 56 (n.d.): 121–55.

38. Gerben Zaagsma, *Jewish Volunteers, the International Brigades and the Spanish Civil War* (Bloomsbury Publishing, 2017). 67 The claim that the games were a Jewish creation is credited to Henry Szulevic, a veteran of the International Brigades, in the footnotes of Zaagsma's book as well as in Arno Lustiger, Daniel Meyer, and Chantal Kesteloot, *"Shalom Libertad!": les juifs dans la guerre civile espagnole* (Paris: Ed. du Cerf, 1991).

39. COOP. "Press Service. English Edition, No. 7," June 29, 1936.

40. Raanan Rein, "El Desafío a Los Juegos Olimpicos de Berlin 1936: Los Atleteas Judios de Palestina En La Frustrada Olimpiada Popular de Barcelona," *Historia Contemporánea* 56 (2017): 121–55.

41. Muriel Rukeyser, "We Came for Games," *Esquire*, October 1, 1974.

42. Clara Thalmann and Paul Thalmann, *Combats Pour La Liberté: Moscou, Madrid, Paris* (La Digitale, 1983).

43. COOP. "Press Service. English Edition, No. 7," June 29, 1936.

44. COOP. "Press Service. English Edition, No. 6," June 18, 1936. Archives of the Trades Union Congress.

45. "Para La Formación Del Equipo Catalán Para El "Trofeo Thalemann"," *El Mundo Deportivo*, April 1, 1930.

46. Muriel Rukeyser, "We Came for Games," *Esquire*, October 1, 1974.

47. COOP. "Press Service. English Edition, No. 5," June 1, 1936.

48. "Press Information." British Workers' Sport Association, June 24, 1936. Archives of the Trades Union Congress.

49. "Press Information." British Workers' Sport Association, June 24, 1936. Archives of the Trades Union Congress.

50. COOP. "Press Service. English Edition, No. 7," June 25, 1936
    According to the COOP they were:

    Al Chakin (Activities Council 80 Fifth Avenue New York). Wrestling Boxing
    Frank Payton (Activities Council 80 Fifth Avenue New York). 100 metres High Jump Broad Jump
    Eddie Krauss (I.L.G.W.U.) High jump, hop step & jump, pole vault, high hurdles
    Dorothy Tucker (I.L.G.W.U.) 100 metres running, long jump, swimming.
    Harry Engel (I.L.G.W.U.) 100 metres, 220 metres, running long jump,
    Bernard Danchik (Williamsburg Gymnastic Group) Gymnastics
    Julian Raoul (French Sports Group) Cycling
    Charles Burley (Unattached) Boxing
    M. Dickies (Activities Council 80 Fifth Avenue New York). Shot Put
    Francis A Henson, Treasurer Committee on Fair Play in Sports
    B Chamberlain, Executive Secretary Committee on Fair Play in Sports

51. Labor Chest for the Relief and Liberation of Workers of Europe, July 1, 1936, Archives of the Trades Union Congress.
52. Muriel Rukeyser, "We Came for Games," *Esquire*, October 1, 1974.
The US team is named by Rukeyser as "Dr Smith and George Gordon Battle in charge and Al Chakin, boxing and wrestling; Irving Jenkins, boxing; Frank Payton, Eddie Kraus, Dorothy Tucker, Harry Engle, Myron Dickes, all track; Bernie Danchik, gymnast; Julian Raul, cycling; Charles Burley, William Chamberlin and Frank Adams Hanson."
53. COOP. "Press Service. English Edition, No. 7," June 25, 1936.
54. Bruce Kidd. "Canadian Opposition to the 1936 Olympics in Germany." *Sport in Society: Cultures, Commerce, Media, Politics* 16, no. 4 (May 1, 2013): 425–38.
55. "British Workers' Sport Association Press Information. Barcelona Popular Olympiad." British Workers' Sport Association, June 9, 1936. Archives of the Trades Union Congress.
56. Muriel Rukeyser, "We Came for Games," *Esquire*, October 1, 1974.
57. The provisional list included

S. JONES (Roath Harriers) Welsh 100 yds Champion.
H. GALLIVAN (Swansea Valley A.C.) Welsh Cross-country Champion and B.W.S.A. national 3-mile Champion.
Gaylard (Mellingriffith S.C.) Welsh 440 yds Champion.
J. Alford (Roath Harriers) Welsh 1/2 mile, and mile, Champion.
Ken Harris (Roath Harriers) represented Wales in mile event at British Empire Games.
E. Sears (Essex Beagles) Essex 880 yds Champion.
J.L. Rees (Swansea Valley A.C.)
R.G. Hopkin (Swansea Valley AC) D. James (Swansea Valley A.C.)
C.G. Cupid (Swansea Valley A.C.). Glamorgan 220 yds Champion, and for many years sprint champion of Wales, and European Workers' sprint champion.
M. Cullen (Swansea Valley A.C.)
C.G. Sim (Elswick Harriers) Northern 220 yds and Long Jump Champion.
L.R. Pearce (Hants 380 yds and mile Champion.
Bernard Bamber, holder for many years of the B.W.S.A. Men's Singles Championship, joint holder of Men's Doubles, winner of the International Workers' Tournament held in Paris, in both Men's Singles and Doubles events.
The National Clarion Cycling also promised two of its leading cyclists to compete in the 100-km event at Barcelona, and other sections of the Clarion are also forming teams.
"BRITISH WORKERS' SPORTS ASSOCIATION. ORGANISING COMMITTEE FOR TEAM FOR BARCELONA PEOPLES' OLYMPIAD," June 24, 1936. Archives of the Trades Union Congress.

58. "British Workers' Sport Association Press Information. Barcelona Popular Olympiad." British Workers' Sport Association, June 9, 1936. Archives of the Trades Union Congress.

59. Rafael Pascuet and Enric Pujol, eds., *La Revolució Del Bon Gust: Jaume Miravitlles i El Comissariat de Propaganda de La Generalitat de Catalunya (1936–1939)*, 1. ed. (Barcelona : Figueres: Arxiu Nacional de Catalunya : Viena Ediciins ; Ajuntament de Figueres, 2006).

CHAPTER 5

The Events

Abstract The events scheduled at the 1936 Popular Olympics go a long way in revealing the intentions of the organizers and what would have been the character of their games. From mass relay races to women's running events that were far more equal with those of men than those in Berlin, they show a commitment to sport for all. This chapter outlines the events that were planned, their location, and their place in the sporting pantheon of the period.

Keywords Athletics • Women's sport • Olympics • Barcelona • Popular sport

In the 800-metre Women's Olympic final in Amsterdam in 1928, nine women lined up to compete. All nine would finish, with six of them beating the World Record in the process. Newspaper reports at the time did not see this athletic spectacle for what it was—a reflection on the athleticism of the women involved and a clear indication that previous contests had not allowed women to achieve what they were clearly capable of. Rather, according to one reporter, "It was not a very edifying spectacle to see a group of fine girls running themselves into a state of exhaustion."[1] Many newspapers reported that competitors collapsed and had to undergo substantial resuscitation. Such was the uproar at the "indecency" of seeing women naturally exhausted after running faster than none in recorded

© The Author(s) 2020

J. Stout, *The Popular Front and the Barcelona 1936 Popular Olympics*, Mega Event Planning,
https://doi.org/10.1007/978-981-13-8071-6_5

history that the event was removed from future games, not to return until 1960.

The events scheduled for a games tell us a lot about the ideology behind it. Ideas of gender, nation, and class are wrapped up in the seemingly unimportant schedules of running races and swimming relays that precede each games. We can see, for instance, the IOC's refusal to allow tennis to enter the games due to its entirely class-based insistence on the model of the gentleman-amateur and subsequent exclusion of paid tennis professionals. We can also see the martial focus of sports governing bodies reflected in events like dressage, modern pentathlon, and shooting. Gender biases are made yet more obvious when women are not permitted to run more than 200 m.

The infrastructure of a games communicates a message as well. From Beijing's Bird's Nest to Berlin's Bell Tower, the architectural setting for an Olympiad communicates how the host wishes to be perceived by the world. Los Angeles built an Olympic village patrolled by cowboys in 1932 and quickly turned it into a real estate development sold to California's growing middle class. Before it became host to the athletes, Berlin's Olympic village hosted an even less desirable set of neighbours, the pilots of the Condor Legion who would go on to pioneer new and modern methods of mass murder at Guernica and throughout Republican Spain. Barcelona, meanwhile, used a stadium that already existed and billeted athletes in homes, hostels, and hotels, wherever they could be held.

In an era where Olympic spectacle was becoming the norm, the Popular Olympics aimed to make their mark on the men and women who came and who left carrying a new message and seeing the world differently rather than in the skyline of the host city or the pocket books of its real estate agents. All of these preparations, in place by the 19th of July, would never see the light of day. But they remain as valuable clues to the tone, content, and character of the Popular Olympics.

Accommodation

The COOP promised to provide all athletes with "free board and lodging for the actual duration of the games,"[2] surely a significant cost for the committee and a substantial incentive for the mainly working-class participants. This lodging was to be a mixture of requisitioned commercial spaces and billets in the homes of supporters. Rukeyser tells of "The Hotel Olympic—immense building requisitioned for the athletes"—this seven-storey edifice would hold about 1600 athletes in close proximity to the events, as the hotel, like the stadia, was originally built for the 1929 Exposition. Rooms would hold four to eight people, and washing facilities would be provided for every 8–12 competitors. Women would stay on one floor or in a separate wing of the hotel.[3]

The stadium itself held another 3000 "spotless bright single rooms" for competitors as well as 72,000 seats for spectators.[4] For the remaining athletes and travelling spectators, further sleeping arrangements were made in the pavilions around Montjuïc which had been set up for the 1929 Exposition. Despite these seemingly watertight preparations, an appeal was made on the 29th of June to the people of Catalonia to make "everything ready for the foreign delegations, to place their quarters at the disposal of visitors, and give all support to preparations going forward."[5] As the number of expected athletes exceeded the rooms available, the city itself would take on the burden. This was a games for the people after all, and it would be the people who hosted their fellow popular athletes.

The Berlin and Los Angeles games had placed athletes from different nations in distinct areas of an Olympic Village; the Barcelona games threw them together. The accommodations reflected the attitude of the organization, which saw not an opportunity for inter-national conflict but rather a chance to build a supernational alliance. National identities, be they state-nations or not, were to be embraced within an atmosphere of a greater fraternity. Catalans, Basques, Moroccans, and Jews without a home would all share dormitories, showers, and a greater identity.

Between all these facilities there would be a network of buses and groups of guides and interpreters, including some Esperanto speakers, ready to aid foreign athletes should they wish to travel around, or leave, the "great settlement" that the Popular Olympics promised to build on the hill of Montjuïc.[6] One imagines the atmosphere among the competitors would have been somewhere between a rally and a summer camp. The week would have been a fantastic opportunity to enact the solidarity that the Popular Front promised.

FACILITIES

The athletic and football events were scheduled for the 72,000-seat stadium atop the hill in Montjuïc. This stadium, which still stands today and hosted the 1992 games, had been built for the 1929 Exposition and was undoubtedly a world-class facility. There would be a running track, facilities for gymnastics and athletics, and a pitch for ball sports. The Metallurgical Palace would hold the chess tournament. Boxing would be spread between a number of sites on or adjacent to the Montjuïc hill (the Greek Theater, Plaza Las Arenas, and the Foixada botanical gardens) as well as the more established boxing venue of Iris Park in the Eixample. Wrestling would have a unique stage, the "*Poble Espanyol*" or Spanish Village, an exhibition at the bottom of the Montjuïc hill that contained houses that were supposed to typify the various regions of Spain for the visitor to the 1929 Exposition.[7]

Swimming events were to be held a short distance away, and the "borough and provincial" athletes would find themselves competing chiefly at Les Corts, the home of FC Barcelona.[8] Football and rugby games would be held at the homes of FC Barcelona and RCD Espanyol, respectively. Longer distance events, such as walking and cycling, would span the city. The former began in Plaza España, at the top of the Ramblas; the latter took a wide circuit but had its start and finish in Montjuïc. Rowing would take place in the port, fitting for a sport with its roots tied to both working-class watermanship and upper-class boating. Meanwhile, those flying acrobatic planes would leave from an aerodrome outside the city.

It is clear that this games would pull in the entire city and stick to the well-established tradition of using stadia and facilities developed for a World's Fair to host a sporting event, but in this case the sports would be far from a sideshow or an exercise in demonstrating white supremacy. Private facilities all around the city were also commandeered, from housing to boxing it would be the citizens of Barcelona who helped provide for their fellow citizens of the Popular Front.

EVENTS

The games were to host a range of events that spanned from a full suite of track and field contests to exhibition games and more unique cultural demonstrations. Overall, there were 41 medals available for elite men, 20 for elite women, 15 for men of the second category, 6 for women of the second category, 5 medals for regional teams, and one medal for women's regional teams. In addition to this, there were 2 exhibition sports (handball and baseball) and a series of dances, songs, and artistic exhibitions which would not be competitive in nature. Some events were listed in the newspaper schedules,[9] but not in the official sporting programme; if these events were added, there were at least two more medals, for archery and rowing, as well as other possible demonstration events such as boules.[10]

In the stadium, traditional running, throwing, and jumping events would take place for both high-level inter-national competitors and less talented athletes. Competitors were to submit their best performances and would be allocated a position in the elite, second-level "provincial," or lowest-tier "borough" contests. Each nation was permitted three individuals or one team in each of the highest-level contests; inscriptions in the second and third categories were unlimited. The best athletes would serve to establish records, not to glorify themselves or their nations but "[to] show the broad masses of people that astonishing feats can be achieved by sporting activity and the training of the body" which would, in turn, serve as "a means of propaganda for the better hygiene and physical training for the peoples, and for creating the conditions for such a training." The other athletes would compete in different races, but share the same meals, hotels, and spirit of solidarity.[11]

Unique to the Popular Olympics were the mass relay races. The most spectacular of these events took place on the opening night in the stadium—it pitted entire national teams against each other in a 20 × 500-m relay race. This race was for regional athletes, but given the size of various delegations, there may well have been non-runners deputized from other sports. There was also a 10 × 100-m relay on the track and a similar contest for men in the pool alongside a 10 × 50-m swimming event for women. These mass relays seem to evoke memories of a school sports day rather than elite performance and would surely have been quite the spectacle. In the spirit of popular sport, they rewarded nations with a healthy and athletic populous who worked well together rather than highlighting individual brilliance. These events, more than any others, would "emphasize the popular character of the games."[12]

Women would also compete across a slightly less numerous set of sprints, jumps, hurdles, and throwing events than men, but could compete in more than three times as many medal events as they could in Berlin. The IOC games restricted women to running events of 200 m and shorter, fearing anything more would be damaging to their delicate constitutions. The Barcelona games included a race of 600 m for women as well as basketball and tennis. It wasn't equality, but it was progress.[13]

A similar system was used in the pool. Elite events would be at the standard inter-national distances and athletes could compete in one of three categories. In addition to the more expected distances, strokes, and diving contests were the demonstrations of nautical rescue techniques and an event for boys under 13 and girls under 14, which was likely a request by the Club Natació Barcelona, which placed a strong emphasis on young people learning to swim on the grounds of safety and public health.[14] Again, the popular character of the games is evident in the placing of sport for public health on the same pedestal as sport for record performance.

Outside of the sporting stadia, a 100-km cycle race as well a shorter criterium race (to be held under lights at night), a 50-km walk, a 25-km run (not the 42.2-km marathon distance which was standardized in 21 and used at the IOC games), and team sports such as rugby, basketball, and football would occur. Combat sports included both Greco-Roman wrestling and boxing. Both combat sports allowed one inter-national competitor per nation per weight category (there were 8 categories) and an unlimited number of competitors who had not competed on the inter-national stage.

The Berlin games included several events that were absent in Barcelona. The equestrian events seem to jar with the class narrative of the Popular Olympics and were an easy omission. Canoeing and sailing may have also been a logistical challenge for teams travelling by train and were likely of limited appeal to working-class athletes. Of the ball sports, handball and baseball were included in the Barcelona games as exhibition events without medals. The same was true for gymnastics, mass variants of which were popular in working-class organizations but which had less following as a competitive sport.

The Barcelona programme included several events that expanded the IOC programme. Rugby and tennis were both included in the Popular Olympics; both were popular sports among the working classes, with the latter excluded due to the IOC's myopic devotion to the "gentleman amateur" model of athletes. Pétanque or boules, known as bocce in the USA, was also included, and its popularity and accessibility are evident to anyone travelling through Barcelona to this day. Basque Pelota, the fastest ball sport in the world, was also included and promised quite the spectacle for the uninitiated attendees.

In addition to adding sports that were not welcome in Berlin, there were a series of activities beyond sport on the Popular Olympic programme. A week-long chess competition was scheduled and seems to have been expecting an inter-national field which would occupy all 800 of the provided boards. Alongside a non-competitive demonstration of traditional dancing and singing from competing nations at the opening ceremony, there would be a series of dancing and singing displays and even an artistic exposition which was to include plastic arts, photography and architecture related to popular sport or "social topics from a progressive standpoint."[15] A writing contest on the theme of popular sport was also included. There was to be a music festival on the opening night that would showcase the musical talents of those attending the games and compositions written for the event. This was the commitment to creating a popular sporting culture that the COOP talked about in its propaganda.

These expanded events were the reason that the Popular Olympics also went by the name of the "Week of Popular Sport and Folklore."[16] Throughout the week there would be events to showcase traditional dances, storytelling, and musical performances from Catalans and their guests. These events were collaborative, not competitive, and would help to create a spirit of solidarity among the attendees and the citizens of Barcelona.

Non-elite Sports

There was a great emphasis on mass participation rather than the record performance in popular sport. As Coubertin had once said, but the IOC had long ceased to believe, "the important thing in the Olympic Games is not to win, but to take part."[17] Certainly, the IOC games may have begun as a sort of transnational bourgeois cultural phenomenon, but by 1936 they had become a battleground for racial ideologies and competing visions of the future. Many in Berlin were under no illusion that they were meeting to do anything other than prove the champion virility of their athletes and, by extension, the superiority of their race and ideology. Barcelona wished to promote a different kind of ideology, one that saw sport as a means to health for all, as a correction to the stresses and strains of industrial labour, and as a means of bringing classes together in the service of a progress that would liberate the people of the world from industrial drudgery and fascist hegemony.

Huge participation was expected in what were termed "provincial and borough" categories. These categories were for athletes who had not posted the fastest qualifying times or scores but still wished to attend the games in order to show solidarity with all that they stood for. As official documents put it, "all, whether first or last class, are serving the idea of free popular sport."[18] Although many athletes from Workers' Sports federations and teams, including some who were planning to compete in Barcelona, would have outperformed medalists in Berlin, these games were not just about them and their performances. Rather, the winners would be the people of the Popular Front, who felt a stronger sense of togetherness and experienced the strength and skill of their anti-fascist brothers and sisters. The games intended that bodies which were once in conflict, and which fascism would have lined up against each other again, would stand together in solidarity. In this they were not wrong; however, they did not expect those bodies to be standing together at the barricades before the sports had even begun.

In the football competition alone, 35 Spanish and 100 Catalan teams planned to compete. They would be joined by French regional FSGT teams and squads from the other regions of Spain and as far away as Mandatory Palestine,[19] and even younger athletes who were permitted to compete in youth events. The goal was to bring people together through sport and improve the well-being and solidarity of the anti-fascist working classes of the world. Where fascism sought to demonstrate the superiority of one man over another, the Popular Olympics wished to demonstrate how they could all live better together.

The mass of athletes would return to the stadium for another mass gymnastic display and parade that would take in all the attending athletes on the final day of the games. Here they would solidify the solidarity and brotherhood they had felt throughout the games. Taking part in a spectacle together would show the world a muscular, healthy, and unified anti-fascist movement. The closing ceremony was to be accompanied by displays of acrobatic flying, the football and archery finals, and the last of the running races.[20] It was this display with which Barcelona hoped to leave the world stage. This feeling of strength and togetherness was one that could be drawn on as the athletes departed to fight fascism at home. Those who would doubt the power of anti-fascism or its ability to defend itself against the hardened Teutonic bodies on display in Berlin would have had their doubts laid to rest at this display of collective solidarity and strength. Sadly, the next time the nations of the world carried their flags through Barcelona was not on the July 1936, but in October 1938, when the beleaguered and battle-weary International Brigades bid farewell to the people of the Spanish Republic and left to carry a very different message home than the one the games had intended.

THE OPENING CEREMONY

The 1932 Olympics in Los Angeles had set records for the crowd size at the opening ceremony. A choir of 1200 led the crowd in the singing of the USA's national anthem and the Olympic hymn, hundreds of doves were released, and the Olympic flame was lit in a giant cauldron. Much of the spectacle associated with opening ceremonies today began in the 1930s with the Hollywood games of 1932 and the Hitler games of 1936.[21]

In Barcelona, preparations were being made for an equally spectacular ceremony that would highlight Catalan artists and the assembled Popular Front nations. The games were to open with a celebration of Catalonia's cultural contribution to the world. Pau Casals, the father of modern cello music, was to conduct an orchestra and choir of 2000 voices in a rendition of the "Hymn to the Popular Olympics," the words for which had been written by Josep Maria de Sagarra. Sagarra perfectly tied the old Catalan nationalism to the new; he had won a prize for his poetry at the *Jocs Florals*, the paramount expression of elite cultural Catalan identity in the early twentieth century. Now his words would serve the new popular Catalan identity and be paired with music written by Hans Eisler, a German composer "who had to leave Germany on account of his race and his free spirit."[22] Each of their contributions would have been useless without the other, but when they came together across national boundaries, they created something greater than the sum of its parts, serving as a symbol for what was possible with an inter-national Popular Front.

This rendition would be followed by a parade of the assembled nations, many of whom were already gathering in the stadium the day before the ceremony was due to begin. Amongst those training, translating, and meeting people from outside his home country for the first time was 16-year-old Eduardo Vivancos. Vivancos spoke Esperanto, an illustration of his incredible capacity for language and devotion to an inter-national conception of Catalan identity. Fifty-six years after Vivancos stood in that stadium, he would recount his experiences there for *Flama*, the publication of the *Casal dels Països Catalans de Toronto* of which he was a member, having lived in Canada when he was forced into exile by the war that would begin that very evening.[23]

Vivancos recounts that the stadium was "a hive of activity" and the atmosphere as "very fraternal." He recalls that few of the visitors spoke Spanish, and that they tried to use newly learnt words, often leading to what he called "amusing interpretations" as botched translations combined with good-natured friendship caused much laughter. Vivancos, who had never spoken directly with foreigners before, also spoke a little French but didn't have much luck in communicating with his fellow athletes as they limbered up in the Montjuïc stadium. Despite his difficulty of being understood, "this experience reinforced for me the conviction that it would be desirable to encourage the spirit of friendship between peoples of diverse ethnicities and nations."

Friendship was not the only sentiment filling the stadium that day. Vivancos notes that there were "alarming rumors of a military rebellion" circulated in the stadium and fomented an atmosphere of tension; however, the Catalan government representatives assured the athletes that all was under control. Just as some young gymnasts had begun their practice routine, one of the organizers announced "some fascists have sabotaged the electrical installations. We'll resolve the problem and it will all be ready for the inauguration of the games tomorrow." Even 56 years later, Vivancos recalled that the announcer's voice seemed "distressed."[24]

That evening, Pau Casals was conducting a final rehearsal of Beethoven's Ninth Symphony which was to be performed the following day by an orchestra and the choir of the *Orfeó Gracienc*, a Catalan institution that played an important role in the elite resurgence of cultural Catalanism, as part of the inauguration of the Cultural Olympiad. An official entered the auditorium to announce that "we are suspending the rehearsal. We have received notice that tonight there has been a military uprising in all of Spain. Both the concert and the Olympiad have been suspended. Everyone leave immediately." Casals, perhaps sensing the gravity of what was to come, announced to the panicked musicians, "I don't know when we are going to see each other again; I propose to you that before we leave each other, we play this symphony together." He lifted his baton and they began playing what would become the anthem of European Unity decades later, the Ode to Joy.[25]

Later, Casals would recall, "we sung the immortal hymn of brotherhood, but in the streets of Barcelona, and in many other cities, they were preparing for a fight that would spill so much blood." And so, they departed, unsure if they would reunite tomorrow to welcome the youth of the world to a future of inter-national unity, or if they would awake to the sound of that future meeting its end at the barrel of a Mauser rifle.[26]

The same rumours were circulating in the stadium where Antoni and Alfons Cánovas were practising gymnastics. The two young Catalans who had been born in Murcia turned to their father for advice; 80 years later, Antoni recalled what his father said: "Do what you believe is right, but always do what is right for the people."[27] For young Antoni this meant joining the militia immediately. Instead of walking out to compete as a swimmer, he marched out of Barcelona towards Zaragoza that same week.

That next morning, the hymn of inter-national solidarity was not the sound that filled the air. At 5:15 in the morning the radio announced: "People of Barcelona, the moment we feared has arrived; the army has betrayed its word and its honor, it has risen against the Republic. For the citizens of Barcelona, the time of great decisions and great sacrifices has arrived. Destroy this fascist army! Every citizen must do their duty! Long live the Generalitat! Long live Catalonia! Long live the Republic!" With this, the games slipped into hindsight and the war assumed its position as the only thing that would matter for the next three years. But, as Vivancos concluded, in these moments we saw "what could have been a great Popular Olympics in Barcelona, prepared with vision and enthusiasm by people of great spirit who believed in Olympic and human ideals."

NOTES

1. Knute Rockne, "Yankees Have Another Dull Day in Olympics," *Pittsburgh Press*, August 3, 1928.
2. COOP. "Manifest, Programa," 1936.
3. COOP. "Press Service. English Edition, No. 7," June 29, 1936.
4. "Press Service. English Edition, No. 6," June 18, 1936. Archives of the Trades Union Congress.
5. COOP. "Press Service. English Edition, No. 7," June 29, 1936.
6. COOP. "Press Service. English Edition, No. 7," June 29, 1936.
7. COOP, "Programa Esportiu de l'Olimpiada Popular," July 1936, Archives of the Trades Union Congress.
8. "Press Service. English Edition, No. 6," June 18, 1936. Archives of the Trades Union Congress.
9. "Un Avance Del Programa Completo de Los Juegos Populares," *El Mundo Deportivo*, July 19, 1936.
10. "Un Avance Del Programa Completo de Los Juegos Populares," *El Mundo Deportivo*, July 19, 1936.
11. COOP. "Press Service. English Edition, No. 7," June 25, 1936.
12. COOP. "Press Service. English Edition, No. 7," June 29, 1936.
13. "Berlin 1936," accessed March 6, 2019, https://www.olympic.org/berlin-1936.

14. COOP. "Press Service. English Edition, No. 7," June 29, 1936.
15. COOP. "Programa Esportiu de l'Olimpiada Popular," July 1936. Archives of the Trades Union Congress.
16. "Un Avance Del Programa Completo de Los Juegos Populares," *El Mundo Deportivo*, July 19, 1936.
17. Peter L. Dixon, *The Olympian* (Santa Monica, CA: New York: Roundtable Pub.; Distributed by Hippocrene Books, 1984).
18. COOP. "Press Service. English Edition, No. 7," June 25, 1936.
19. COOP. "Press Service. English Edition, No. 7," June 25, 1936.
20. "Un Avance Del Programa Completo de Los Juegos Populares," *El Mundo Deportivo*, July 19, 1936.
21. David Goldblatt, *The Games: A Global History of the Olympics* (WW Norton & Company, 2018).
    B. J. Keys, *Globalizing Sport: National Rivalry and International Community in the 1930s* (Harvard Univ Pr, 2006).
22. COOP. "Press Service. English Edition, No. 7," June 29, 1936.
23. Eduardo Vivancos, "Los Otros Juegos Olímpicos de Barcelona," accessed August 31, 2018, https://www.nodo50.org/esperanto/artik33es.htm.
24. Eduardo Vivancos, "Los Otros Juegos Olímpicos de Barcelona," accessed August 31, 2018, https://www.nodo50.org/esperanto/artik33es.htm.
25. A translation of Vivancos' work can be found at nodo50, a publication of the Asociación Izquierda y Esperanto—Eduardo Vivancos, "Los Otros Juegos Olímpicos de Barcelona," accessed August 31, 2018, https://www.nodo50.org/esperanto/artik33es.htm.
26. Eduardo Vivancos, "Los Otros Juegos Olímpicos de Barcelona," accessed August 31, 2018, https://www.nodo50.org/esperanto/artik33es.htm.
27. "Antoni Cánovas i Lluís Martí Bielsa," Ara.cat, July 17, 2011, https://www.ara.cat/cronica/Antoni-Canovas-Lluis-Marti-Bielsa_0_518948101.html.

CHAPTER 6

After the Games

Abstract Although the Popular Olympics never occurred, in a sense they met many of their goals. The coup which launched the civil war failed in Barcelona, but it succeeded in much of the rest of Spain, and for many of the dedicated anti-fascists of the Popular Olympics, this provided a long-awaited chance to take up arms against their old foe. This chapter traces the national and individual contributions to the International Brigades that have their roots in the Popular Olympics.

Keywords Popular Front • International Brigades • Spanish Civil War • Barcelona

The only shots that athletes had expected to hear that July day were those of the starters' pistols. Instead, the city around them rang out with the Mauser rifles and Hotchkiss machine guns of the Guardia Civil, the rag-tag armaments of the workers' militia, and the replies of the Spanish military, who had begun their coup just as the would-be Olympians were arriving. So closely tied were the two events that Popular Olympic posters appear in photos of the barricades that were thrown up that morning. Fortunately for the Republic, workers' militias and the police were better prepared than their guests and had been organizing for the coup for several days. The military, perhaps believing its own myth of superiority, was not prepared for the scale and organization of resistance and failed to take

© The Author(s) 2020
J. Stout, *The Popular Front and the Barcelona 1936 Popular Olympics*, Mega Event Planning,
https://doi.org/10.1007/978-981-13-8071-6_6

control of Catalonia's capital. Barricades emerged in the streets, and anarchists, communists, and Catalan nationalists stood side by side against those who were attempting to subvert democracy.

A Belgian competitor recalled that

> the streets were empty under a burning sun (…) In the Plaza del Comercio we came across the first barricades (…) a few hundred meters further away were armed syndicalists (…) Barricades appeared every hundred meters with all the lateral streets blocked off… We slid along the fronts of the buildings as bullets flew across the square. Instinctively we took refuge in a doorway. We clearly saw the snipers in the bell tower of the church shooting the workers on the barricades in the back.

However, despite the surprise and fear that must have overwhelmed the visiting athletes, they were also impressed with the strength of the resistance to the coup. French FSGT official and correspondent Auguste Delaune would report for the periodical *Sport* that "the Catalan and Spanish people cannot be defeated!"[1]

Alongside the barricades which sprung up on the day Barcelona should have been celebrating the first day of the Popular Olympics were the issues of *El Mundo Deportivo* that had been printed the night before. On the front page they carried photographs of the athletes training for a gymnastic spectacular that was to be hosted in Montjuïc that night along with lists of teams and events.[2] It was not until the 23rd, after some athletes had attempted to stage ad hoc individual events, that Jaume Miravitlles would officially cancel the games.[3]

Much of what was heroic about 1936 has been forgotten, overwhelmed perhaps by the events of the next decade, but nonetheless deserving of a place in both history and popular memory. Jesse Owens, the black sprinter who briefly outran Nazi hatred to win not only gold medals but the hearts of the world that summer, died impoverished in 1980. Likewise, the International Brigades, the 35,000 young men and women who came from around the world to stand up for democracy, have been largely lost to history. In the USA, those who fought the same battle that their nation would undertake in 1941 were labelled as "premature antifascists" and faced the loss of their freedom and citizenship when they returned home from the battlefields of Spain.[4] Many lost more. Nearly half the volunteers never returned to their home countries as the International Brigades repeatedly found themselves in the thick of the fighting against a foe they considered to be the enemy of all mankind.[5]

The Popular Olympics were a casualty of that first day of the Spanish Civil War. However, their participants remained largely unscathed. Some attempted to hold their events once the shooting had stopped; others wholeheartedly intended to return in October, once the regrettable issue of the seemingly defeated coup had been dealt with. All the athletes at the games had come to fight fascism in some way. For some that battle was one they were ready to fight on the playing field and not the battlefield. Others had already seen where the path that the coup pointed to would lead and were more than prepared to stand up to it. For the Germans and Italians, fighting fascism in the streets must have seemed more tempting than a life of exile or hiding. For the French, the decision was between fighting in Spain or going home to prepare for total encirclement by the adversary they had come to show their opposition to. The British and the US contingent were torn between a war that they clearly had a side in but didn't have to fight, and governments at home that seemed determined to bury their heads in the sand until fascism came knocking on their own doors. Facing the prospect of arrest at home if they stayed, many elected to leave. More than a few, however, decided to stay despite the risks and used the ideological and physical preparation they had undertaken for the games to more directly combat fascism.[6]

In the chaos that ensued, some undoubtedly slipped away to the north. French and British steamers were able to enter and leave Barcelona in the days after the conflict began, and many athletes from both nations returned home to tell the story of what they had seen on the streets of Barcelona. In the triumphant atmosphere of the cities that had repulsed the coup, foreigners committed to the cause of anti-fascism let their support to the Republic and joined the militia.[7] A number of athletes, perhaps seeing the impending conflict in Europe or perhaps swayed by the sense of inter-national fraternity before the games, announced their intent to stay at least long enough to hold a march against fascism,[8] and many relocated to safe hotels and waited for what looked like a short-lived and failed coup to fizzle out.

The early days of the civil war were a vision of the goals of much of the European left. The city, "jewel like,"[9] according to journalist Muriel Rukeyser, who was stuck there with the athletes, served as something of an egalitarian utopia, albeit one without much food, electricity, or safety. It was the workers who had saved democracy and the workers who controlled the city. Industries were nationalized, vehicles expropriated from the homes of the plotters. Militia columns were formed from the various unions, and the Popular Front took on a physical form as the columns marched off to Zaragoza. The barricades that sprung up in the hours following the coup were an illustration of the power of the Popular Front to unite the working class and defend their interests and the power of that united working class to hold their own against a military that was not only better armed but also better supported by its allies in Germany and Italy.

Soon, the same solidarity networks that had allowed for athletes from around the world to rush to Barcelona were back in action carrying news of the coup and the response to it. Working-class organizations, newspapers, and parties sent out the call for volunteers and were met with an eager response. Meanwhile, bourgeois governments vacillated and ultimately pursued a policy of non-intervention that denied the Republic the supplies it needed to survive the conflict. Much like the games themselves, the gaps in government support were filled by the organizations of working-class inter-nationalism, and the eager bodies of the young workers of the world began to flow across the Pyrenees again. Both of them came close to success, and maybe even to changing the world, but both ultimately failed.

Adopted Catalans

Many of the Catalans and Spaniards who were competing in the games enlisted immediately. For some, this meant fighting to defend their homes. For others, this meant separation from their families and homes which was not that different from the inter-national athletes. Unlike their comrades from outside Iberia, these Spanish Popular Olympians couldn't go back home to safety and democracy and were left with no choice but to fight.

For those who were stuck in a republic that had ceased to exist in their hometowns, the only way to get home was to seize their homes back for the Republic. These Spaniards from Aragon and Mallorca who were stuck in Catalonia would have been in good company with their choice of socialist, anarchist, anarcho-syndicalist, and communist groups to join arms with. They were joined in the militia by Catalans, such as Antoni Cánovas and Eduardo Vivancos, who had been in the stadium the night before practising an entirely different set of manoeuvres. The young Catalans whose reflections gave us such a vivid account of the preparations for the games would both survive the war and outlive the Francoist regime that took away what would surely have been a defining moment of their youth. Most who joined those early Catalan militia would not survive the war. After a misadventure in Zaragoza and the bloody siege of Madrid, those who survived were forced into the regular military and from there into exile or prison if they survived the fighting.

THE INTERNATIONAL BRIGADES

The inter-national economic depression that hastened the rise of fascism had destabilized old realities around the globe; from Washington to Warsaw, many workers felt that the collapse of the global economic system showed that it was time for a new political order in which the fruits of modern industry were more equitably distributed. Left-leaning groups looked to the Spanish Republic as a beacon of the possible. It was in previously backward Spain that 7000 schools were built in a year,[10] land was beginning to be more equitably distributed, great artists like Lorca engaged with working-class literacy, the Church had been removed from its pedestal, and women were advancing in their political and social rights. As Orwell said, "the working class were in the saddle"[11] and the world watched them with interest. When this North Star of popular politics faced being snuffed out by forces firmly rooted in the old order, it was not only the people of Spain who felt compelled to rush to its defence.

In a technical sense, anyone who remained after the Popular Olympics could not have joined the International Brigades as they did not exist. Rather, the first inter-national volunteers to fight for the Republic, as *Treball*[12] and *La Vanguardia*[13] reported, simply enlisted in the Popular Militia. These anti-fascist volunteers organized units called *Centuria* to denote their fighting force of roughly 100 soldiers. These Centuria included the German *Thalemann Centuria*, the Italian *Gastone Sozzi Centuria*, the British Tom Mann Centuria, and the French *Commune de Paris Centuria*. Each was named for heroes or high points of the people's movement up to this point, believing that they carried the legacy of their forebears and that they too would go down in history. Later, these units would provide the names and structure for the International Brigades.

The International Brigades were not officially formed until October 1936 when the Soviet Union began to support the efforts of Italian and French Communist Parties to send a column of soldiers over the Pyrenees. Stalin, in an attempt to both catch up with and control the spontaneous flow of anti-fascist volunteers, contributed over 500 communists living in exile in the USSR as well as equipment and arms through the Comintern. Using the Centuria as a nucleus where possible, the volunteers who were protecting Madrid were organized into largely language-based battalions. Some volunteers, such as Eric Arthur Blair (better known by his pen name of George Orwell), did not share the Stalinist interpretation of Marxism often enlisted in Catalan or Spanish militias more aligned to their viewpoint. Overall, of the 40,000 non-Iberian volunteers who came to defend the Republic, about 5000 would fight outside of the International Brigades.[14]

By December 1936, there were five International Brigades, numbered from 11 to 15. Battalions were often national in character, but many mixed volunteers who shared a language; the British battalion included members of the Irish Free State, for example, and the Canadian Mackinze-Pappineau Battalion was, at times, mostly composed of US citizens. This combination of adventurers, ideologues, and exiles would ultimately fail in their mission to defeat Franco, but they would go down in history, largely thanks to the multitude of writers in their midst, as the defenders of democracy.

It is important to understand the International Brigades as a global phenomenon but one with European roots. Even the thousands who came to fight from North America were primarily immigrants, fighting the last battle in a war which had seen them flee their homelands. The brigades were composed of ideologues, veterans from labour struggles around the world, and experienced soldiers who had fought in the First World War and the Irish War of Independence and on the streets of Germany and Italy. As Graham has said, "it is impossible to understand the International Brigades as a phenomenon without taking into account their origins in European diaspora."[15] This experience of conflict granted them more combat experience than many Spanish units, and thus they were often used as shock troops and suffered huge casualty rates (the first iteration of the German Thalemann battalion, for instance, was entirely wiped out in the defence of Madrid). The Brigades were part of the army that held Madrid in 1936, and with this action, and those at Jarawa, Guadalajara, Terfel, and the Ebro, they prolonged the life of the Republic by several years.

The nations from which these volunteers came often refused to support their efforts. In February, the League of Nations banned foreign volunteers from travelling to Spain and French police arrested would-be soldiers as they crossed the border. Many returned home unsure if they would keep their citizenship, or their freedom. Jobs were hard to come by for the "premature antifascists" of the Abraham Lincoln Brigade in the USA, and the Canadian "Macc-Papps" and Swiss brigadiers were imprisoned for their efforts to protect democracy.[16] Later, some would find themselves in the front lines of the same battle in a different country as they enlisted in the Second World War.

Long before the International Brigades were even a thought, the Popular Olympians found themselves thrust into a physical manifestation of the ideological struggle they had all been coming to fight. Accounts of the first few days of the conflict vary hugely, as one would expect given the chaotic nature of events. It can be hard to trace many of the participants of the games as they are often not listed in the pre-event communications. Some stayed, some left, and some left and then returned. In those first few weeks, foreign men and women enlisted in the Catalan militia alongside local workers. Many of their stories may never be told, but the few that I have found make for moving reading and an insight into the brave athlete-soldiers who jumped into action at a moment's notice to defend a democracy that they had known for just days against a threat they had seen coming for years.

RUKEYSER

Muriel Rukeyser was a young but talented poet who had made a name for herself by covering the Scottsboro Case in which nine black teenagers were convicted of rape by an all-white jury despite a lack of evidence. Rukeyser, on her first trip across the Atlantic, was planning to serve as an assistant to a couple writing books about cooperatives in Northern Europe. However, once in London, she began to spend time with leftist journalists and politicians and, through these connections, received an assignment to cover the games when her more senior journalistic colleagues were invited to a wedding. Undoubtedly the young reporter was hoping for a life-changing opportunity, but she couldn't have guessed what lay ahead as she boarded a train heading south to Barcelona. What began as sports reporting quickly became much more as her train was stopped in Montcada, within earshot of the shooting in Barcelona.[17]

With surprise, she dismounted the train and took refuge as columns of smoke and rifle fire erupted from the south. Her earliest reporting noted that that "these are not Spaniards; they are Catalans," but also took pleasure in the fact that "there is actually a united front now in Catalonia, Socialists, Communists, Anarchists, all backing the government." After some time being stuck outside of the city, "The party cars arrived and all those connected with the Workers' Olympics were taken in open trucks... Our Suitcases were piled up for fortification; we were told to duck when shot at." Finding herself embroiled in the conflict, she noted that "two thousand foreigners, thrown on the city as the Civil War began, are to be lodged and fed here. The stadium is filled with athletes and stranded nationals."[18] Rukeyser's accounts, which are spread between several poems, articles, and a novel, are perhaps the best source available to recount what the Popular Olympians experienced in the initial days of the civil war, and they help us give some structure to the decisions those athletes made regarding whether to depart or remain.

Athletes from Rukeyser's train, and those arriving via other modes of transport, were shuttled to the Hotel Olympic, where they slept on mattresses on the floor. Even the officials who had been ready to welcome them were occupied, "tearing up paving stones for barricades."[19] Athletes were ferried around in vehicles stained with the blood of their previous occupants by the same people who had seen the previous occupants of those seats die. Yet they also saw the city come alive as workers occupied barricades and their Catalan hosts presented a vision of a less authoritarian military and a revolutionary future in which men and women fought side by side for a society in which they could live as equals.

Rukeyser describes meetings in the stadium at which Monsieur de Piche, a French minister sent to observe, states his intent to leave with his team in order to remove the burden of caring for them from the Republic. The French then left the next day from the port after one of their athletes was killed. Rukeyser noted that the general feeling was in support of this move. France was facing complete encirclement and "we all felt that the Popular Front in France and Spain must be preserved at all costs."[20] The French team departed on two boats, singing the Internationale as they left.

Those athletes who stayed a few days longer marched in a huge parade with the militia, headed by bagpipers from the British team and black armbands for those who had died; they marched through the Ramblas singing the Internationale in various languages. At a meeting, the assembled athletes were given a way to serve the Republic even as they left it: "you have come for the games, but you have remained for the greater Front, in battle and in triumph. Now your task is clear; you will go back to your countries and spread through the world the news of what you have seen in Spain."[21] This would be the role Rukeyser herself took on, along with many of her comrades.

Athletes were later asked to vacate the hotel and make their own arrangements in the city. The US consulate offered them "safe conduct" but without the offer of boats; this meant a suicidal car trip, which most declined. Rukeyser notes that the consulate didn't recognize the team as it was not an official Olympic squad but nonetheless advised them to remove jewellery and formal clothing to appear more proletarian. When HMS London arrived from Gibraltar to extract British nationals, they were not allowed on board. Many US citizens, including Rukeyser, joined the Belgians on *Ciudad de Ibiza*, a ship operating at double its capacity, and left the Republic.[22] Notably, Rukeyser saw that it was felt by the people of Catalonia that "America would surely be a friend of the Republic,"[23] but this was not to transpire.

Not all of those who came to compete were on the boats that left in the chaotic days following the coup. The parade, which is confirmed by *La Vanguardia* and *Treball*, was followed by a tough choice for many athletes. Although most left to share the stories of Catalan anti-fascism with their fellow countrymen, *La Vanguardia* reported that "many of the foreign representatives have enlisted in the militias."[24] Rukeyser likewise noted that "some of the athletes are talking of joining the fighting forces," including one German athlete named Otto who had been living in exile in Paris before the games and attended alone. The German workers, whom Rukeyser counted as "at least ten," as well as a Hungarian and a Belgian, who had faced persecution at home for their political affiliations, found a home in Catalonia, where their views belonged, and they represented their nation.[25]

In these early days of chaos, it seems incredible that any of the visitors did anything other than flee the country that had erupted into war as soon as they arrived. But for many, this was a war that they had already begun, and Spain offered much better odds of success than they had at home. And so, they lent their bodies and often their lives to making Spain the place that the Popular Front put a definitive stop to fascism. Sadly, the rest of the world would see Spain as the place that their non-intervention could put a definitive stop to communism.

THE USA

The US team, which is named in the correspondence, is one of the easier teams to track. There were a total of around 2800 volunteers from the USA who fought in the Spanish Civil War, many of them with a history of union activism and anti-fascism at home. These volunteers would serve in various units but would be collectively remembered as the Abraham Lincoln Brigade.

Al "Chick" Chakin, a Cornell graduate and wrestler who was working on his MA, left for the Popular Olympics as the US team's coach and to compete as a wrestler and a boxer. On the outbreak of war, he returned home with the rest of his squad and became an advocate for the Republic. However, he found himself uncomfortable giving speeches back in New York, while his hosts in Barcelona took up arms for a cause he believed in. So, he elected to return as soldier. His wife, knowing that he had problems with a frequently dislocated knee, pondered whether to tell the doctors who signed his medical examination certificate, but decided not to, feeling that this was his choice and an important action.[26] Chakin enlisted in the Canadian Mackenzie Papineau battalion where he served as quartermaster and regularly wrote to his wife. She was able to send him knitted scarves and chocolates, and he was able to tell her of the people and landscapes of Spain. In Early 1938, her letters stopped receiving replies until he was declared missing in action on March 17, 1938.[27]

Chakin's teammates also did their part for the Republic. Frank Payton, a black sprinter, addressed huge crowds at Madison Square Garden as part of a fundraiser for the Republican forces. Francis Henson, the treasurer of the committee for Fair Play in Sports, helped to organize medical aid for the loyalist forces and was joined in this effort by Muriel Rukeyser. The USA would go on to contribute a large amount of material and human support to the Republic, with collections funding ambulances from the same groups who had, a few years before, worked to boycott the Berlin Olympics.[28]

BRITAIN

The British support for the games was an important addition to the parade of nations scheduled to take part in the events as the government of the UK was not part of the Popular Front. Despite disagreements between politicians, more than 2200 men and women left Britain to fight for the Spanish Republic.[29] British workers had long had a strong relationship with their unions, and those unions felt a deep connection to the their co-ideologues in Spain who they saw as part of a struggle against privileged aristocrats and an established church which they themselves shared.

Although it is not possible to find any of the athletes named in the TUC's correspondence in the International Brigades, there do seem to be several volunteers whose presence is, in some way, attributed to the Popular Olympics.

Bill Alexander, a British Commissar in the International Brigades and member of the Communist Party of Great Britain, mentions George Hardy in his memoirs. Hardy was a member of the British Workers' Sport

Federation and had travelled to Barcelona with the British team,[30] but left when they were taken back to Britain as a group and then returned later as a volunteer on January 7, 1937.[31] Hardy was a print worker by trade and served in the International Brigades until he was killed by a sniper on March 31, 1938.[32]

Irish volunteer Phil Gillan is recorded as being in Barcelona "for" the Olympics with the British delegation. It is not clear exactly what role he was playing there but he also seems to have returned home before returning to Spain in September 1936 (his date of arrival in Spain is recorded as September 19). Gillan served as a driver with the Tom Mann Centuria, a small group of British volunteers, including Peter Spencer, aka Viscount Churchill, and two touring cyclists who happened to have been in Spain at the time that the fighting began.[33] After participating in a botched raid on Mallorca, the Centuria saw little action and welcomed their incorporation into the Thalemann Battalion in October of 1936. Gillan served alongside the British and German volunteers before being wounded and returning home in February 1937.[34]

Aileen Yvonne Palmer, an Australian child of writers Vance and Nettie Palmer, was just 21 in 1936, and was working as a translator at the Popular Olympics. A prolific writer herself, much of what she witnessed is catalogued through the extensive archive of diaries and letters presented in the excellent biography *Ink in Her Veins*. Palmer had arrived earlier that year along with her family and picked up a job with the COOP, writing their publicity material in English and German. It is likely her translations which informed much of this text in the form of archived press releases and letters. On the 18th of July, she stayed with friends and tried to get tickets for her parents to watch the opening ceremony. She was awakened by friends and took great delight in seeing the victory of the Republic. "The Government of Catalunya passed out what arms it had to the workers who lined the streets, and, even without arms the workers rose, tore up paving stones, built barricades and fought.... we were as happy as if the fate of all Spain had been decided that day."[35] Her parents, living further away from the city, had assumed the shots they heard were part of the Olympic ceremony, but when they found out about the conflict, they came looking for their daughter, only to find her busy translating messages for the athletes who wished to send telegrams home. On the 28th of July, Aileen was told by her parents that the family was leaving. Despite securing a letter from the local militia ensuring their safety, the family had decided, and she left along with her parents on the 29th on a British warship.[36]

Aileen returned quickly, arriving in Spain again on the 2nd of September, to streets that she declared had a "ragged look" about them. She began as an orderly at the British Hospital in Grañén, a small town that was an anarchist stronghold and had done away with money entirely. Kenneth Sinclair-Loutit, a Cambridge-educated anti-fascist who ignored a threat of disinheritance from his father to serve as head of a British medical unit in Spain, was appointed in charge of the unit. This bizarre group set about establishing a hospital in a farmhouse where Loutit and Peter Spencer would try to work alongside the local moustachioed mayor who carried a pistol and went by Pancho Villa. Quickly, Palmer was established as Loutit's assistant and secretary as well as the group's translator in terms of local politics as well as language.[37]

Palmer's secretive and obsessive diary-keeping often saw her suspected of spying by the other British medical team who were highly divided along political lines. Eventually, Palmer was deployed to the Aragon front with her unit, and then, as they were absorbed into the International Brigades, she was sent to Albacete and Brunete. After nine months at the front with virtually no rest, she returned to the UK and recovered before making the choice to go back to Spain despite the horrendous amount of death she had seen in her position as a nurse. She served at Teruel, and then in Barcelona as the Republic was split in two by Franco's forces, before eventually leaving Spain in the summer of 1938. She would return again to help the Spanish people in refugee camps in France before serving as an ambulance driver in the London Blitz. In her later life, she would work as a poet and writer, but her sexuality and mental health issues would see her subjected to electroconvulsive therapy and insulin shock treatment.[38]

Loutit's reflections on the situation could have spoken for his secretary as well as all the other volunteers:

> We were mostly young, we were not yet really battle-hardened, though, by now, we had all had a sufficient experience to know what war really meant. We were certainly ready to carry on, we were convinced that our side in the Spanish Civil War was as right as the other was wrong. Even more determinant to our morale was our profound belief, irrespective of our nationality, that we were fighting for the future of our own homelands; I then believed (as I do today) that Spain's fight was not just for the values that we in England took for granted, it was against forces that were directly antagonistic to Britain. 1939/1945 proved us right but, in 1937, our premature anti-fascism was not always understood.[39]

Sport also continued to link the Spanish and British left. Lewis Clive, who had won a Gold Medal in the 1932 Los Angeles games as a rower, died at the battle of the Ebro in 1938.[40] The British Trades Union Congress attempted to send a football team in March 1937 to represent British unions against Catalonia. The British Foreign Office refused to allow them to travel, even at their own risk, on grounds of non-intervention. It was noted by the Generalitat that these athletes could expect nothing less than the "unvarying courtesy" that the British popular athletes had encountered in July 1936.[41]

IRELAND

Ireland sent volunteers to fight on both sides of the war. On the right, there was a strong opposition to the Spanish Republic because of the perceived hatred the Republic had of the Catholic Church. Eoin O'Duffy, leader of the fascist National Corporate Party, took 700 volunteers to join Franco's forces. The Irishmen achieved little, mostly being used as a political token but finding themselves unable to measure up to the Francoist ideals of "Spanishness." The Irish Brigade suffered its heaviest casualties in a friendly fire incident and shortly thereafter refused to advance and was withdrawn from the front.[42]

The Irish International Brigadiers embodied a true sampling of the nation's identity groups, from Communist to Catholic and Orangeman to Republican. A total of 320 went. Some felt Ireland was under threat from fascism, others went as part of unions, and still more as they felt this was an extension of Ireland's own conflict and wished to bury old scores with both O'Duffy's troops who had long been the enemy. They were retroactively known as the Connolly Column but often found themselves dispersed between the British and American battalions, depending on their willingness to serve alongside soldiers who had, in at least one case, previously been Black and Tans in a different war.[43]

Bill (Willoughby) Scott, a protestant bricklayer whose father had fought in the well-organized and trained Irish Citizen Army in the 1916 Easter Rising and who had himself fought with the Irish Republican Army, had travelled to the games to represent a free and independent Ireland. He had, presumably, had his fill of authoritarian regimes and the repression of national identity after being imprisoned in British military custody in 1934, and he elected to remain in Spain at the outbreak of hostilities. His letters home were published in working-class newspapers and served to motivate his fellow Irishmen of all political stripes to join him.[44]

Scott fought in the Tom Mann Centuria, where he served as Political Commissar before joining the Thalemann Battalion and with them defending Madrid due to his sincere conviction that "a victory for fascism in Spain is a victory for fascism in Ireland."[45] Wounded in the neck, he returned home to raise funds and to stand for election as a candidate for the Communist Party of Ireland but was withdrawn as a candidate in favour of Republican leader Frank Ryan. This gave him time to make a second trip to Spain and receive a serious leg wound that caused him to be repatriated. He resigned his Communist Party membership over the Molotov-Ribbentrop pact, but later rejoined the party in 1941. From then until his death in 1988, he would appear writing letters to editors and giving interviews to try and prevent the loss of the memory of his comrades in arms.[46]

FRANCE

It may have been France that sustained the first inter-national casualty of the Spanish Civil War. A French athlete was killed on the day of the coup when the safe passage that had been granted to the visiting teams was violated and he was shot[47] and others wounded by an airborne attack.[48] Most French athletes found themselves back in Perpignan in a matter of days, and had nothing but praise for "the workers' militias of Barcelona who were protecting us French tourists from the terrorists."[49]

France played an important role in sustaining the Spanish Republic even if Blum's government was not willing to send military support in an official capacity. Even after signing the non-intervention pact, Blum continued to supply the Spanish Republic with aircraft, pilots, and engineers. It was through France that many of the inter-national volunteers travelled on their way to the conflict, using a network of sympathetic safe houses and support. France also contributed the most volunteers of any nation, around 9000 in total,[50] even after the threat of fascism to France itself became clear. When the war was lost, it was to France that many fled, fearing the reprisals that would characterize the victory of the rebels.

Given the size of French involvement in the Popular Olympics and the International Brigades, it would be surprising if there were not some overlap; however, it has been challenging to find any examples without lists of the French Popular Olympians. What is clear is that links between French-sporting bodies and their Catalan colleagues persisted even during the war. The Magazine *Sport* maintained correspondence with the FSGT before and during the conflict. Both parties read each other's publications, and the Catalans eagerly awaited the news of the growth of popular sport in France even as their own young people were engaged in a bloody conflict. Both groups shared the political goals of "preparing the Catalan youth for a future which is free and happy." Even as the Republic was in peril, its athletes and their representatives still forged links with the Popular Front abroad.[51]

GERMANY

As Borkenau related, many on the German left wished "to wash away the ignominy of their defenseless retreat before the forces of Hitler"[52] by striking a blow against fascism in Spain. Initially, 15 Germans formed the core of what would become the Thalemann Centuria. The group was named for a German communist killed by the Gestapo three years earlier.[53] Thalemann had also given his name to the first inter-national sporting event that the CCEP hosted, the *Copa Thalemann* in April 1936.[54] Soon they were joined by many more of their countrymen including the approximately 66 German anarchists who had been living in exile and elected to fight with the CNT/FAI Durruti Column. The Thalemann column's German volunteers included refugees from the outlawed Communist Party along with Jewish refugees who wanted to take the fight to fascism with the hope of one day fighting the same enemy at home.[55] As Graham relates, even songs from early Nazi prison camps made their way to Spain with the anti-fascist exiles.[56]

By August 1937, before the International Brigades existed, the German Communist Party was calling for volunteers for the front. Soon the Germans would form multiple battalions and find themselves leading the charge against their old foe. In many cases, this was more than an ideological battle; German government forces aided Franco's nationalists from the outset of the war, giving the German volunteers for the Republic a chance to face off against the same Nazis who had driven them out of their home country. In their first month of combat, roughly half of the German volunteers were killed defending Madrid. Some of them no doubt by their own countrymen who were using the Spanish capital as a testing ground for modern bombing techniques.[57]

Despite these setbacks, and multiple changes in command, the German contingent fought bravely and was one of the most numerous nationalities in the International Brigades, with over 5000[58] serving the Republic at some point during the conflict. Following the battle of the Ebro when some inter-national units took casualties of up to 75%, it was agreed that the volunteers would leave Spain in October 1938. For the Germans, there was often nowhere to go. Many ended up in France, where they would fight fascism again in the resistance or face years of forced labour in prison camps, others were welcomed into the Soviet Union, and many lived out their lives in exile.

Rukeyser reports hearing from the athletes, mostly German, who left with the first militia columns headed to Zaragoza; presumably, these were the initial Thalemann group. She recounted that "their morale is strong and people's front is invincible"[59] as it must have seemed in August 1936. Amongst these men was Otto Boch, who Rukeyser described in an obituary she wrote for him 35 years later as a "Bavarian, runner, cabinet maker. Fighter for a better world.[60]" Rukeyser first met Boch in Montcada where her train was stopped by the beginning of the conflict. Their romance quickly blossomed and clearly impacted Rukeyser a great deal as he appears in her poetry, and as a character in *Savage Coast*, her novel about the early days of the war.

Boch seems to have enlisted in the Thalemann Centuria.[61] Rukeyser, in her article about the first days of the War for Esquire, recounted his instant decision to stay and fight. When the war broke out, "[i]t was certain for Otto. He had found his chance to fight fascism... it was the German chance, in or out of Germany."[62] Boch remained with his unit through various reorganizations until he died on the banks of the Segre River in 1939; this was after the official return of the International Brigades, but Germans like Boch had no home to return to and likely remained in the Republican army.[63]

Boch was not the only German athlete to stay and fight. Clara Thalmann had come to swim, but she also found herself at the barricades in those early days. Thalmann, and her partner Pavel, strongly opposed Stalinism and enlisted in the anti-Stalinist *Partido Obrero de Unificación Marxista* (POUM) where they would help produce German-language propaganda broadcasts before joining fellow Germans in the anarchist Durruti column.[64]

The couple would go on to join the Friends of Durruti, a group that fought against regularization of the militia under the Comintern's influence in the infamous "May Days" of Barcelona 1937. Thalmann, and other decided anti-Stalinists, remained committed to the revolution even during the war, while the socialist, communist, and bourgeois nationalist left wished to impose order on the militia and the population. Eventually, these disagreements boiled over, and 500 were killed and 1000 injured in what is often called "the civil war in the Civil War."[65] The atmosphere of suspicion and tension leading up to these events makes up much of the plot of Orwell's *Homage to Catalonia*. Thalmann found herself caught up in this fighting and sharing a rooftop with Orwell, who had also enlisted in the POUM militia.[66]

The Thalmanns attempted to flee by boat shortly after the May events and were captured. Fortunate enough to be in contact with friends in Switzerland, they were released and moved to Paris, where they were both active in the resistance during the Second World War.[67]

POLAND

It was not only political exiles who had fled to Barcelona in the early 1930s. Zaagsma[68] estimates that there were "a couple of thousand" Jews in exile in Barcelona at the outbreak of the civil war. Many came from Poland, where anti-Semitism rose dramatically during the economic depression.

Polish Jewish footballer Emmanuel Mink,[69] who had been living in Antwerp, found his way into the civil war as volunteer after arriving to play for a Jewish team (likely the *Yiddisher Arbeter Sport Klub* or YASK) in the Popular Olympics.[70] Later he would become a leader in the all-Jewish Botwin Company of the Polish Dombrowsky Brigade.[71] Mink had nowhere to go when the International Brigades were returned home, so he and many other "Botwins" joined the *Agrupación Internacional* (international group) and covered the retreat of civilians towards the French border at the end of the war. Mink himself fled across that border, only to be interred in a concentration camp in France and later sent to a German camp where he joined up with other former volunteers from around Europe and the Middle East in the camp's underground movement. Later, Mink and other Jewish communists would be purged from the Polish party in a wave of anti-Zionist sentiment that followed the Six-Day War. These purges would cause Mink and others to flee again, this time to France. In France, Mink campaigned for the restoration of pensions to himself and his comrades and was joined by the British and the US former volunteers; sadly, he was unsuccessful.[72]

Mink was not alone in carrying the flag for the YASK. One member, Yaschar Aronowicz, was active in the *Parizer Yidiser Arbeter Teater* (Parish

Yiddish Workers' Theater) group. Presumably, he came to Barcelona for the cultural Olympiad before he joined the militia.[73] Newspaper correspondent T. Elski wrote for *Naye Prese*, a Yiddish-language communist newspaper published in Paris. It was through Elski's writing that many of the Jewish leftists in exile discovered the role played by their comrades in the struggle. Elski's work set the volunteers in an inter-national conflict, and helped frame the struggle as against anti-Semitism. Elski was joined by other Jewish volunteers in the Thalmann Centuria. His bravery, and that of the volunteers he recruited when he returned to France to speak or who were inspired by his articles, helped dispel the anti-Semitism that some in the European left had clung to.[74]

ITALY

Germans were not the only political exiles in Barcelona in the summer of 1936. In the early days of the war, *Treball* carried notice of the "hundreds" of Italian exiles who sent support to those who had enlisted alongside the Catalan proletariat to fight fascism.[75] Many of these Italians would have been already living in Barcelona, unable to return home due to their political or social opinions; they took advantage of Spain's relatively generous visa and asylum provisions to shelter amongst their fellow ideologues. Their first grouping was known as the Gastone Sozzi Centuria and formed in September 1936; new volunteers and the Centuria's survivors would later become the Garibaldi Battalion. It is unclear how many of the initial volunteers in the Centuria were athletes and how many were exiles from outside the games or those who came from France to join the fight in the first weeks of the conflict.[76]

AUSTRIA

For some of the athletes, there was no time to enlist with a formal military unit. They arrived in the country to see what they had seen at home, armed insurrection and the pitting of the military against the people. Unlike other European countries, Catalonia had an armed, trained, and prepared working class. Seeing the Catalan unions take to the streets and push back their own military must have been inspiring for many of their guests, so much so that some immediately sprung to the aid of their hosts and fought a battle they had been waiting for years to have a chance to fight.

Jaccod Menchter, an Austrian athlete, who was one such spur-of-the-moment volunteer, was killed in an attack on the Atarazanas barracks where many of the coup plotters were garrisoned. German and Austrian exiles living in Barcelona played a vital role in the first 36 hours of the conflict. Many of them had been keeping tabs on their Nazi countrymen, and as soon as the shooting started, they began a deeply personal mission, that of capturing or killing those who had forced them out of their homeland. The *Gruppe Deutsche Anarcho-Syndikalisten im Ausland* (Group of German Anarcho-syndicalists in Exile or DAS) captured the Barcelona German Club and found there a machine gun, numerous other weapons, and lists of Nazis in Spain. Even before the International Brigades had been formed, foreign volunteers had struck a crucial blow for the Republic.[77]

PALESTINE

One of the more remarkable teams in Barcelona was that of Mandatory Palestine. Evidently unwelcome at Berlin and, despite British oppression, the home of a strong Workers' Sport movement, Barcelona was the obvious choice for the Zionist left which was largely represented by the Workers' Sport organization Hapoel. The Palestinian delegation was made up of 21 ideologues who opposed both bourgeois sport and fascism and whom their own governing body described as "muscular and combat experienced."[78] Many decided that fighting fascism in Spain might be the beginning of liberating Europe from the anti-Semitic ideology which was threatening to make the continent a no-go zone for an ethnic group who had been resident there for centuries.

Estimates suggest that 3500–4000 of the inter-national volunteers in Spain were Jewish.[79] In the early days of the civil war, Jewish media carried announcements of the hostile attitudes towards Judaism that the Nationalist rebels held. This, combined with a high number of culturally Jewish people in the European left, soon saw a significant arrival of Jewish volunteers. Later, the media in Palestine would downplay this contribution in order to keep young fighting men at home, only to recover their memory in the decades after the Second World War. For some young men in the Communist Party, British expulsion left them no choice and they joined the European left diaspora that began arriving in Spain in 1936.[80] Although the Botwin Company was entirely Jewish, and even published a Yiddish newspaper at the front during the conflict, the majority of Jewish soldiers were distributed throughout the International Brigades, fighting as anti-fascists first and foremost.[81]

The Palestinian delegation's arrival and fate is documented in a recent article by Raanan Rein.[82] The group found themselves trapped in a train at Portbou when the war commenced. When their delegation leader, Israel Carmi, arrived in Barcelona by motor car, he was confronted with a scene resembling a slaughterhouse. Most of the Palestinian team left quickly via Marseilles, but even as the last of them attempted to cross the Pyrenees heading north, they met those coming south to fight for the Republic that had welcomed Jewish exiles back to Europe. Despite the promises that Carmi had made to their mothers to return them safely, some remained and launched themselves immediately into great danger.

Footballer-turned-referee Chaim Elkon, a member of the prohibited Palestinian Communist Party, had moved to Palestine in 1924 after a football tour and was joining the team in Barcelona as a referee, having been exiled from Palestine for his political beliefs. He was not a member of Hapoel but appears to have been a convinced anti-fascist as he joined Austrians and Germans in the Thalemann Centuria when the war broke out and headed to Madrid where the fighting was fiercest. Like almost all of his unit, Elkon never returned. He was killed in the fierce fighting near the University City when his unit was surrounded, and he attempted to use a submachine gun to cover the escape of his comrades.[83] Elkon was joined by another exile, Nachum Weiss (who had a number of synonyms in his work with the Palestinian Communist Party). Weiss joined the Edgar André column, named for another communist detained by the Nazis. Weiss would also not survive the first year of the war. He died in November 1936.[84]

Imre Jacobi, another footballer who had stayed in Palestine after arriving there on a sporting tour with his club Hagibor Bratislava in 1927, was the most famous of the athlete-soldiers from Palestine. Jacobi was something of a star player, having scored a decisive goal in the 1933 Palestine Cup. Riding his Norton motorcycle around between games, always with a new companion riding pillion, he was quite the David Beckham of interwar Mandatory Palestine. His brother, an established lawyer and musician in the UK, would always see him as something of a blight on the family name. When he wasn't out chasing women on his motorcycle, it appears that Jacobi was deeply involved in the communist movement. A search of his apartment by British authorities revealed several false passports, which led to his arrest and expulsion from Palestine in June 1936.[85] Without a home to go to, he too made the decision to join the Popular Militia. Rein has suggested that many other members of the Jewish left might have faced a similar choice between imprisonment and fighting for the Republic.[86]

Jacobi took his love of motorcycles to the front where he eventually met his demise. He was struck by a mortar bomb while carrying orders to the front near Jarama, one of the fiercest battles of the first phase of the conflict, and after being transported to a hospital near Madrid, he died and was buried there.[87]

CONCLUSIONS

In the days after the games, Barcelona must have been a scary and exciting place for the Popular Olympians. Other foreign nationals, aligned more with the interests of capital than the people of Catalonia, fled the city by any means available to them. But many in the Hotel Olympic wished to stay, if not to fight, then to observe a city which had come under the control of the working class. Many planned to return for a games which was promised in October.[88] They thought that the coup would have been swept away by the autumn and the events would serve not as a demonstration of the power of the Popular Front, but as a celebration of what it had already achieved. Others tried to compete in the days after the coup, but did so with little support from the organizers or other competitors. Many more sat in hotels, hostels, and embassies, as well at the streets and squares of the city, trying to find out what was going on, get news to families, and revel in the realization that the power in the city lay with the people in its streets.

Most of the athletes who came to Barcelona remain anonymous. Lost in union archives or in documents that did not survive the Franco dictatorship, but the fragments of the stories we have help to give an insight into the incredibly brave, committed, and diverse group of people who gave a face and a body to the Popular Front. It is through these fragments that we can piece together a picture of what the games promised to be, and what they could have shown the world were they not overshadowed by war.

The trajectories of the Popular Olympians were as diverse as their backgrounds. For some, what was supposed to be a week-long trip to Barcelona lasted the rest of their lives, and for most, their experiences there shaped the rest of their lives. The potential of the games to create alliances and shape identities could not have been more emphatically demonstrated than it was in July 1936. Orwell famously called sport "war minus the shooting,"[89] but as he would later observe himself, the ties built through sport were more than strong enough to endure when the conflict did come to include shooting.

NOTES

1. Ruben Castelló Mateo, "Patrimonio Histórico Español Del Juego y Del Deporte: La Olimpiada Popular de 1936," *Museo Del Juego*, 2011.
2. "Un Avance Del Programa Completo de Los Juegos Populares," *El Mundo Deportivo*, July 19, 1936.
3. Muriel Rukeyser and Rowena Kennedy-Epstein, *Savage Coast: A Novel* (New York City: The Feminist Press, 2013).
4. John Gerassi, *The Premature Antifascists: North American Volunteers in the Spanish Civil War, 1936–39: An Oral History* (New York: Praeger, 1986).
5. Casualty rates were as high as 75% in some engagements. The Thälmann battalion, which refused to retreat under fire in the defence of Madrid, lost two whole companies in 1937 and yet is barely remembered when we think about Germany in the 1930s.
6. Beevor places the total of those who remained at 200 A. Beevor, *The Battle for Spain: The Spanish Civil War, 1936–1939* (Penguin Group USA, 2006).
7. "Una Legió d'honor." *Treball*, July 22, 1936.
8. "Nota Important." *Treball*, July 22, 1936.
9. Muriel Rukeyser, "We Came for Games," *Esquire*, October 1, 1974.
10. Douglas W. Richmond, "The Politics of Spanish Financial and Economic Policies During the Second Republic, 1931–1933," *The Historian* 49, no. 3 (1987): 348–67.
11. George Orwell. *Homage to Catalonia*. Mariner Books, 1952.
12. "Una Legió d'honor," *Treball*, July 22, 1936.
13. "Informacion Catalana," *La Vanguardia*, July 24, 1936.
14. Dave Hann, *Physical Resistance: A Hundred Years of Anti-Fascism (John Hunt Publishing, 2012)*.
15. Helen Graham, *The Spanish Civil War: A Very Short Introduction*, Very Short Introductions (Oxford; New York: Oxford University Press, 2005). P. 42.
16. Daniele Mariani, "No Pardon for Spanish Civil War Helpers," SWI swissinfo.ch, accessed February 17, 2019, https://www.swissinfo.ch/eng/no-pardon-for-spanish-civil-war-helpers/6445388.
17. Muriel Rukeyser, "We Came for Games," *Esquire*, October 1, 1974.
18. Muriel Rukeyser, "We Came for Games," *Esquire*, October 1, 1974.

19. Muriel Rukeyser and Rowena Kennedy-Epstein, *Savage Coast: A Novel* (New York City: The Feminist Press, 2013).
20. Muriel Rukeyser and Rowena Kennedy-Epstein, *Savage Coast: A Novel* (New York City: The Feminist Press, 2013).
21. Muriel Rukeyser, "We Came for Games," *Esquire*, October 1, 1974.
22. Muriel Rukeyser, "We Came for Games," *Esquire*, October 1, 1974.
23. Muriel Rukeyser, "We Came for Games," *Esquire*, October 1, 1974.
24. "Informacion Catalana," La Vanguardia, July 24, 1936.
25. Muriel Rukeyser, "We Came for Games," *Esquire*, October 1, 1974.
26. Noel Buckner, Mary Dore, and Sam Sills, *The Good Fight: The Abraham Lincoln Brigade in the Spanish Civil War*, 1984.
27. "Abraham Alfred Chakin." Abraham Lincoln Brigade Archives, n.d. http://www.alba-valb.org/volunteers/abraham-alfred-chakin.
28. Peter N. Carroll, *The Odyssey of the Abraham Lincoln Brigade: Americans in the Spanish Civil War* (Stanford, Calif: Stanford University Press, 1994).
29. Richard Baxell, *British Volunteers in the Spanish Civil War: The British Battalion in the International Brigades, 1936–1939* (Routledge, 2004).
30. Richard Baxell, "The British Battalion of the International Brigades in the Spanish Civil War 1936–1939" (London School of Economics and Political Science, 2001).
31. Bill Alexander, *British Volunteers for Liberty: Spain 1936–1939*, First edition (London: Lawrence & Wishart Ltd., 1984).
32. "Printworkers Honoured," *INTERNATIONAL BRIGADE MEMORIAL TRUST*, February 2003.
33. Richard Baxell, *British Volunteers in the Spanish Civil War: The British Battalion in the International Brigades, 1936–1939* (Routledge, 2004).
34. Richard Baxell, "The Volunteers," http://www.richardbaxell.info/volunteers/.
35. Sylvia Martin, *Ink in Her Veins: The Troubled Life of Aileen Palmer* (Apollo Books, 2016). P. 137.
36. Sylvia Martin, *Ink in Her Veins: The Troubled Life of Aileen Palmer* (Apollo Books, 2016). Quotation from p. 127.
37. Tom Buchanan, *Britain and the Spanish Civil War* (Cambridge, U.K.; New York, NY, USA: Cambridge University Press, 1997).
38. Sylvia Martin, *Ink in Her Veins: The Troubled Life of Aileen Palmer* (Apollo Books, 2016).
39. Kevin Brown, "For Whom the Bell Tolls," *ICSM Gazette*, Spring 2017.
40. Richard Baxell, "The British Battalion of the International Brigades in the Spanish Civil War 1936–1939" (London School of Economics and Political Science, 2001).
41. Generalitat de Catalunya. Comissariat de Propaganda. "Press Release. No. 194: English Edition," March 23, 1937. Archives of the Trades Union Congress.

42. Robert A. Stradling, *The Irish and the Spanish Civil War, 1936–39: Crusades in Conflict* (Manchester University Press, 1999).

43. Michael O'Riordan, *Conolly Column: The Story of the Irishmen Who Fought in the Ranks of the International Brigades in the National-Revolutionary War of the Spanish People, 1936–1939* (Pontypool: Warren & Pell, 2005).

44. Barry McLoughlin, *Fighting for Republican Spain 1936–38* (Barry McLoughlin, 2014).

45. "Ireland and the Spanish Civil War—Police Report on SPNI Meeting on Spain, April 1937," accessed September 13, 2018, http://irelandscw.com/ibvol-ScottSPNI.htm.

46. Barry McLoughlin, *Fighting for Republican Spain 1936–38* (Barry McLoughlin, 2014).

47. Muriel Rukeyser, "We Came for Games." *Esquire*, October 1, 1974.

48. M. D. Benavides, *Guerra y Revolución En Cataluña:(Reportaje)* (Ediciones Tenochititlan, 1946).

49. "Aux Frontières d'Espagne," *L'Humanité*, July 26, 1936, https://gallica.bnf.fr/ark:/12148/bpt6k406786n.

50. Helen Graham, *The Spanish Civil War: A Very Short Introduction*, Very Short Introductions (Oxford; New York: Oxford University Press, 2005).

51. "Borrador de Carta Per a La FSGT," n.d., Unio Esportiva Sants.

52. Franz Borkenau, *The Spanish Cockpit: An Eye-Witness Account of the Political and Social Conflicts of the Spanish Civil War* (London: Phoenix, 2000).

53. Arnold Krammer, "Germans against Hitler: The Thaelmann Brigade," *Journal of Contemporary History* 4, no. 3 (April 1, 1969).

54. "Los Festivales Proximos Del Comité Cátala Pro Esport Popular," *Mundo Deportivo*, March 30, 1936.

55. Arnold Krammer, "Germans against Hitler: The Thaelmann Brigade," *Journal of Contemporary History* 4, no. 3 (April 1, 1969).

56. Helen Graham, *The Spanish Civil War: A Very Short Introduction*, Very Short Introductions (Oxford; New York: Oxford University Press, 2005). P. 43.

57. Arnold Krammer, "Germans against Hitler: The Thaelmann Brigade," *Journal of Contemporary History* 4, no. 3 (April 1, 1969).

58. Arnold Krammer, "Germans against Hitler: The Thaelmann Brigade," *Journal of Contemporary History* 4, no. 3 (April 1, 1969).

59. Muriel Rukeyser, "Liberty Versus Death in Spain." *New Masses*, September 1, 1936.

60. Muriel Rukeyser and Rowena Kennedy-Epstein, *Savage Coast: A Novel* (New York City: The Feminist Press, 2013). P. xxix.

61. Muriel Rukeyser and Rowena Kennedy-Epstein, *Savage Coast: A Novel* (New York City: The Feminist Press, 2013). P. xxvii.

62. Muriel Rukeyser, "We Came for Games," *Esquire*, October 1, 1974.
63. Muriel Rukeyser, "We Came for Games." *Esquire*, October 1, 1974. P. 307.
64. Clara Thalmann and Paul Thalmann, *Combats Pour La Liberté: Moscou, Madrid, Paris* (La Digitale, 1983).
65. Helen Graham, "'Against the State': A Genealogy of the Barcelona May Days (1937)," *European History Quarterly* 29, no. 4 (October 1, 1999): 485–542.
66. Clara Thalmann and Paul Thalmann, *Combats Pour La Liberté: Moscou, Madrid, Paris* (La Digitale, 1983).
67. Gerd-Rainer Horn, "In Stalin's Secret Barcelona Jail," in *Letters from Barcelona: An American Woman in Revolution and Civil War*, ed. Gerd-Rainer Horn (London: Palgrave Macmillan UK, 2009), 183–201, https://doi.org/10.1057/9780230234499_8.
68. Gerben Zaagsma, *Jewish Volunteers, the International Brigades and the Spanish Civil War* (Bloomsbury Publishing, 2017).
69. Mink often went by "Mundek" and his name is often rendered as Mincq in French.
70. Arno Lustiger "Emanuel Mink, Une Figure de La Guerre Civile Espagnole," *Le Monde*, April 10, 2008, https://www.lemonde.fr/disparitions/article/2008/04/10/emanuel-mink-une-figure-de-la-guerre-civile-espagnole_1033116_3382.html.
71. Arno Lustiger, Daniel Meyer, and Chantal Kesteloot, *"Shalom Libertad!": les juifs dans la guerre civile espagnole* (Paris: Ed. du Cerf, 1991).
72. Gerben Zaagsma, *Jewish Volunteers, the International Brigades and the Spanish Civil War* (Bloomsbury Publishing, 2017). 110–13, 125–129.
73. Annette Aronowicz, "Yaschar: My Father's Life In Yiddish Theatre" *Digital Yiddish Theatre Project*, accessed March 5, 2019, https://yiddish-stage.org/yaschar-my-fathers-life-in-yiddish-theatre.
74. Gerben Zaagsma, *Jewish Volunteers, the International Brigades and the Spanish Civil War* (Bloomsbury Publishing, 2017). 74 Zaagsdma makes great use of Naye Prese in his work and provides insight into the role played by Elski and his writing.
75. "Els Italians Antifeixistes Exiliats a Barcelona," *Treball*, July 22, 1936.
76. Carmela Maltone, "Les Antifascistes Italiens Dans La Guerre d'Espagne: Histoire et Mythe de La Brigade Garibaldi," in *Garibaldi : Héritage et Mémoire* (Toulouse, France: Centre Interuniversitaire de Recherche sur l'Italie, 2007), https://hal.archives-ouvertes.fr/hal-01316524.
77. "The Foreign Legion of the Revolution: German Anarcho-Syndicalist and Volunteers in Anarchist Militias during the Spanish Civil War—Dieter Nelles," libcom.org, accessed September 7, 2018, http://libcom.org/library/the-foreign-legion-revolution.

78. Raanan Rein, "El Desafio a Los Juegos Olimpicos de Berlin 1936: Los Atleteas Judios de Palestina En La Frustrada Olimpiada Popular de Barcelona," *Historia Contemporánea* 56 (2017): 121–55.
79. Gerben Zaagsma, *Jewish Volunteers, the International Brigades and the Spanish Civil War* (Bloomsbury Publishing, 2017). P. 2.
80. Raanan Rein, "A Belated Inclusion: Jewish Volunteers in the Spanish Civil War and Their Place in the Israeli National Narrative," *Israel Studies* 17, no. 1 (2012): 24–49.
81. Gerben Zaagsma, *Jewish Volunteers, the International Brigades and the Spanish Civil War* (Bloomsbury Publishing, 2017).
82. Raanan Rein, "El Desafio a Los Juegos Olimpicos de Berlin 1936: Los Atleteas Judios de Palestina En La Frustrada Olimpiada Popular de Barcelona," *Historia Contemporánea* 56 (2017): 121–55.
83. Raanan Rein, "El Desafio a Los Juegos Olimpicos de Berlin 1936: Los Atleteas Judios de Palestina En La Frustrada Olimpiada Popular de Barcelona," *Historia Contemporánea* 56 (2017): 121–55.
84. Raanan Rein, "Echoes of the Spanish Civil War in Palestine: Zionists, Communists and the Contemporary Press," *Journal of Contemporary History* 43, no. 1 (2008): 9–23.
85. Raanan Rein, "El Desafio a Los Juegos Olimpicos de Berlin 1936: Los Atleteas Judios de Palestina En La Frustrada Olimpiada Popular de Barcelona," *Historia Contemporánea* 56 (2017): 121–55.
86. Raanan Rein, "A Belated Inclusion: Jewish Volunteers in the Spanish Civil War and Their Place in the Israeli National Narrative," *Israel Studies* 17, no. 1 (2012): 24–49.
87. Raanan Rein, "El Desafio a Los Juegos Olimpicos de Berlin 1936: Los Atleteas Judios de Palestina En La Frustrada Olimpiada Popular de Barcelona," *Historia Contemporánea* 56 (2017): 121–55.
88. Muriel Rukeyser and Rowena Kennedy-Epstein, *Savage Coast: A Novel* (New York City: The Feminist Press, 2013).
89. George Orwell, "The Sporting Spirit," *The Collected Essays, Journalism and Letters of George Orwell* 4 (1968): 1945–50.

CHAPTER 7

Conclusions

Abstract On July 18, 2016, in the Palau De La Música Catalana, the Orfeó Gracienc assembled to finish a concert that had begun 80 years earlier. Their predecessors had sung Beethoven's Ninth Symphony in Montjuïc under the instruction of Pau Casals, but the military insurrection meant their voices, and the hymn of universal brotherhood they were singing, would never be heard by the world. As Casals fled the city that night and the shots rang out behind him, he declared his intent to conduct the "Ode to Joy" after the conflict finished. Casals never managed to fulfil his desire, but 80 years to the day after he and the choir parted company, they once again launched into the verse which had been the last many of the former choristers would sing together "*Abraceu-vos, oh! milions! Petó de la Humanitat! Brinda celestial bondat*" (get up you millions! The embrace of humanity provides heavenly blessings).

Keywords Pau Casals • Catalonia • Sport • Anti-fascism

On July 18, 2016, in the Palau De La Música Catalana, the Orfeó Gracienc assembled to finish a concert that had begun 80 years earlier. Their predecessors had sung Beethoven's Ninth Symphony in Montjuïc under the instruction of Pau Casals, but the military insurrection meant their voices, and the hymn of universal brotherhood they were singing, would never be

© The Author(s) 2020
J. Stout, *The Popular Front and the Barcelona 1936 Popular Olympics*, Mega Event Planning,
https://doi.org/10.1007/978-981-13-8071-6_7

123

heard by the world. As Casals fled the city that night and the shots rang out behind him, he declared his intent to conduct the "Ode to Joy" after the conflict finished. Casals never managed to fulfil his desire, but 80 years to the day after he and the choir parted company, they once again launched into the verse which had been the last many of the former choristers would sing together "*Abraceu-vos, oh! milions! Petó de la Humanitat! Brinda celestial bondat*" (get up you millions! The embrace of humanity provides heavenly blessings).[1]

A different tune set the volunteers of the International Brigades in their way in October 1938. As they shuffled along the same streets of Barcelona that those first volunteers had walked along two years before, they sung the Internationale, waved their flags, and lined up to hear the Olympian rhetorical abilities of Dolores Ibárruri, known as *La Passionaria*. She finished her speech to the assembled 13,000 brigadiers with a hopeful outlook for the Republic. "You can go with pride. You are history. You are legend. You are the heroic example of the solidarity and the universality of democracy... We will not forget you; and, when the olive tree of peace puts forth its leaves, entwined with the laurels of the Spanish Republic's victory, come back!"[2] It would be another 40 years before any of them could. But in the meantime, the CCEP would be carrying the flag for popular Catalonia in exile. It operated from France until at least 1948 and attempted to secure a boycott of the Franco regime in inter-national sporting events.[3]

Eighty years later, a small and entirely unremarkable football club in the London borough of Clapham took orders for their away kit. Non-league teams struggle to sell tickets let alone merchandise, but the Clapham Community Football Club saw over 5400 pre-orders in just a few days. The shirt, bearing the colours of the flag of the Spanish Second Republic, the slogan "*No Pasaran*" (they shall not pass), and the three-pointed star of the International Brigades, was so popular that orders had to be paused and volunteers mobilized to fulfil demand. In response to unprecedented interest, the shirt's manufacturer, a small Italian brand who support ethical manufacturing and make apparel for clubs fighting against inequality, said, "We strongly believe some battles can be fought both on and off the pitch."[4]

The unabashedly political use of sport surely offended some, but just as was the case in the 1930s, sport is and has always been political. Those International Brigadiers fortunate enough to have survived both Franco's and Hitler's attempts to kill them would surely have supported the working-class people of London using their most powerful cultural export to express their feelings. With fascism and anti-fascism moving from the fringes to the centre stage of the political debate in the USA and the UK, there has never been a more apt time to use the playing field as a podium.

Catalonia too has seen a return to the debates of the previous century. The Franco dictatorship has passed, and Josep Antoni Trabal, the one-time chairman of the COOP, was able to return from exile and stand for election. However, Catalonia still finds itself in conflict with Madrid. At the time of writing, Catalonia's leaders are again locked up or in exile, and the streets of Barcelona, on October 1, 2017, took on a passing resemblance to those of October 1934 as police used tear gas, illegal rubber bullets, feet and fists to keep Catalans from voting on independence from Spain. Having gained substantial autonomy in Spain's post-dictatorship, many Catalans wished to be consulted in the future of their nation's relationship to Spain. Madrid declared their vote illegal, arrested its architects for sedition, took direct control of the nation's affairs, and forced a Catalan election. At times of crisis, the Catalan people turn to their spiritual centres, the Sagrada Familia and the Camp Nou. FC Barcelona, playing behind closed doors on the day of the vote, donned their training shirts (which are essentially the Catalan Flag) for photos before the game and, in a move that would surely have piqued Avery Brundage's rage, released a statement supporting the right of the Catalan people to vote.[5]

Much of what could be said about the legacy of the 1936 games is summed up in these anecdotes, and those that could be told about the 1968 Olympics, Colin Kaepernick and the NFL, and Serena Williams in professional tennis. Sport remains a powerful place for protest, especially by groups who are only valued by society for their bodies. The Popular Olympics have been largely missed out of this trajectory of sporting protest that began when Peter O'Connor climbed a flagpole in the 1906 intermediate games[6] to raise an Irish flag, and continue to this day. The Olympics are in every sense inter-national; they move between nations and host conflict and cooperation between the identity groups which give structure to humanity. When we watch the Olympics, we have to decide who we are supporting, which team we are on. The whole world watches as exceptional human bodies do exceptional things and then uses those experiences to structure their new realities. In recent years, we have seen sports and politics return to the forefront of inter-national consciousness—be it Russia subverting doping rules, Rio funding a stadium instead of schools, or NFL players being vilified for demanding the basic rights of citizenship in a democracy. In this climate, there are important lessons to be learnt from an Olympiad that aimed to unite the world against many of the forces that continue to divide it.

Today the Olympics are a giant commercial spectacle, billions of dollars are spent, and the whole world watches. In recent years, the dramatic increase in cost has seen the games become the preserve of authoritarian states once again. Just as Hitler did in 1936, so Russia and China have jumped at the chance to show their organizational prowess and state power almost a century later. For an organization built on the cultural unity of the transnational bourgeoisie, this oligopolistic market is perhaps not surprising. But for a dream that once offered the people of the world a chance to play together, it is somewhat saddening.

Barcelona finally hosted its games in 1992, and the events were hosted at the stadium on top of the Montjuïc hill that had waited for the athletes of the world in 1936. In 2001, the stadium was renamed for Lluís Companys. Barcelona successfully placed itself at the centre of the world in 1992, and showcased its progressive identity with Paralympic athletes featured in opening ceremonies, and as it had aimed to do in 1936, it allowed the world to play together as former Soviet republics made their various Olympic debuts just a javelin's throw from where the athletes of the 1936 sheltered in their hotel, looking at the city exploding beneath them.

Divisions within sport and society remain profound and seem to be growing, as they must have in 1936. Sport is neither inherently right nor left, neither divisive nor inclusive; rather, it is a tool that can be used to bring people together or push them apart. But the example of the Popular Olympics is an important one as it reminds us that sport retains the ability to build bridges in a world that is building walls. We continue to look to sport for heroes, and to give a structure to our identities and to both reflect and shape our realities. Those heroes, and identities, could be far worse that those who came to Barcelona under different flags and would have raced in different colours, but left as part of the same team.

NOTES

1. Elianne Ros, "El Concert Més Llarg de La Història," *La Vanguardia*, July 16, 2016, https://www.lavanguardia.com/encatala/20160717/403269006730/el-concert-mes-llarg-de-la-historia.html.
2. Richard Baxell, *British Volunteers in the Spanish Civil War: The British Battalion in the International Brigades, 1936–1939* (Routledge, 2004).

3. X. Pujadas and C. Santacana, "The Popular Olympic Games, Barcelona 1936: Olympians and Antifascists," *International Review for the Sociology of Sport* 27, no. 2 (1992).
4. Martin Belam, "'No Pasarán': Spain Laps up Clapton CFC's Anti-Fascist Football Kit," *The Guardian*, August 31, 2018, sec. UK news, https://www.theguardian.com/uk-news/2018/aug/31/no-pasaran-clapton-cfc-anti-fascist-football-kit-proves-hit-in-spain.
5. "FC Barcelona Statement," October 1, 2017, https://www.fcbarcelona.com/club/news/2017-2018/fc-barcelona-statement-1-october-las-palmas.
6. David Goldblatt, *The Games: A Global History of the Olympics* (WW Norton & Company, 2018).

Correction to: The Popular Front and the Barcelona 1936 Popular Olympics

James Stout

Correction to:

James Stout, The Popular Front and the Barcelona 1936 Popular Olympics, Mega Event Planning, doi.org/10.1007/978-981-13-8071-6

The book was inadvertently published without the cover credit line and the same has been updated later. The cover credit line of this book is ©nemesis2207/Fotolia.co.uk

---

The online version of the original book can be found under
https://doi.org/10.1007/978-981-13-8071-6

© The Author(s) 2020
J. Stout, *The Popular Front and the Barcelona 1936 Popular Olympics*, Mega Event Planning,
https://doi.org/10.1007/978-981-13-8071-6_8

BIBLIOGRAPHY

Alvarez, S., and M. D. C. Loredo. *Historia Política y Militar de Las Brigadas Internacionales: Testimonios y Documentos.* Compañía Literaria, 1996.

Borkenau, Franz. *The Spanish Cockpit: An Eye-Witness Account of the Political and Social Conflicts of the Spanish Civil War.* London: Phoenix, 2000.

Buchanan, Tom. *Britain and the Spanish Civil War.* Cambridge, UK; New York, NY, USA: Cambridge University Press, 1997.

Carroll, Peter N. *The Odyssey of the Abraham Lincoln Brigade: Americans in the Spanish Civil War.* Stanford, CA: Stanford University Press, 1994.

Casanova, Julián. *The Spanish Republic and Civil War.* Cambridge; New York: Cambridge University Press, 2010.

Collins, Tony. *Sport in Capitalist Society: A Short History.* Routledge, 2013. https://doi.org/10.4324/9780203068113.

Ealham, C. *Class, Culture, and Conflict in Barcelona, 1898–1937.* Routledge, 2005.

Goldblatt, David. *The Games: A Global History of the Olympics.* WW Norton & Company, 2018.

Gounot, A. "El Proyecto de La Olimpiada Popular de Barcelona (1936), Entre Comunismo Internacional y Republicanismo Regional." *Cultura, Ciencia y Deporte*, no. 3 (2005): 115.

———. "L'Olympiade Populaire de 1936–Substitut Des Jeux Olympiques Ou Spartakiade Déguisée?," in Manifestations Sportives, Mises En Scènes Politiques. Constantes et Variations Dans l'espace International Depuis Le XIXe Siècle, by André Gounot, Denis Jallat, and Benoît Caritey, 2007.

© The Author(s) 2020
J. Stout, *The Popular Front and the Barcelona 1936 Popular Olympics*, Mega Event Planning,
https://doi.org/10.1007/978-981-13-8071-6

Gounot, André. "Sport or Political Organization? Structures and Characteristics of the Fran International, 1921–1937." *Journal of Sport History* 28, no. 1 (2001): 23–40.

Graham, Helen. *The Spanish Civil War: A Very Short Introduction.* Very Short Introductions. Oxford; New York: Oxford University Press, 2005.

Guttmann, Allen. *The Games Must Go on: Avery Brundage and the Olympic Movement.* New York: Columbia University Press, 1984.

Hargreaves, J. E. R. *Freedom for Catalonia?: Catalan Nationalism, Spanish Identity, and the Barcelona Olympic Games.* Cambridge Univ Pr, 2000.

Hill, C. R. *Olympic Politics.* Manchester Univ Pr, 1996.

Kanin, D. B. *A Political History of the Olympic Games.* Westview Pr, 1981.

Keys, B. J. *Globalizing Sport: National Rivalry and International Community in the 1930s.* Harvard Univ Pr, 2006.

Kidd, B. "The Popular Front and the 1936 Olympics." *Canadian Journal of the History of Sport and Physical Education* 11, no. 1 (1980): 1–18.

Large, D. C. *Nazi Games: The Olympics of 1936.* WW Norton & Company, 2007.

———. *Nazi Games: The Olympics of 1936.* WW Norton & Company, 2007.

McDonogh, Gary W. *Good Families of Barcelona: A Social History of Power in the Industrial Era.* Princeton University Press, 1986.

McLoughlin, Barry. *Fighting for Republican Spain 1936–38.* Barry McLoughlin, 2014.

O'Riordan, Michael. *Conolly Column: The Story of the Irishmen Who Fought in the Ranks of the International Brigades in the National-Revolutionary War of the Spanish People, 1936–1939.* Pontypool: Warren & Pell, 2005.

Preston, P. *The Coming of the Spanish Civil War: Reform, Reaction, and Revolution in the Second Republic.* Psychology Press, 1994.

Pujadas et Santacana. "Les Années Trente et La Crise de l'olympisme La Proposition de l'olympiade Populaire de Barcelone (1936)." *STAPS: Revue Des Sciences & Techniques Des Activites Physiques & Sportives* 14, no. 32 (October 1993): 79–86.

Pujadas i Martí, Xavier. *Atletas y ciudadanos.* 1st ed. Alianza Editorial Sa, 2011. http://www.libros.universia.es/Libro-ATLETAS-Y-CIUDADA NOS/9788420664637/493945.

Pujadas i Marti, Xavier. "De Atletas y Soldados. El Deporte y La Guerra Civil Española En La Retaguardia Republicana (1936–1939)." *Estudios Del Hombre,* no. 23 (2007): 89–117.

Pujadas i Martí, Xavier. *Història Il·lustrada de l'esport a Catalunya.* Barcelona: Columna; Diputació de Barcelona, 1994.

Pujadas, X., and C. Santacana. "The Popular Olympic Games, Barcelona 1936: Olympians and Antifascists." *International Review for the Sociology of Sport* 27, no. 2 (1992): 139.

Pujadas, Xavier. *Catalunya i l'olimpisme.* 1st ed. Barcelona: Coc Catalan, 2006.

———. "Del Barrio Al Estadio. Deporte, Mujeres y Clases Populares En La Segunda República, 1931–1936 (Pp. 125–167)." *Atletas y Ciudadanos. Historia Social Del Deporte En España* 2010 (1870).

Pujadas, Xavier, and Santacana i Torres. "Prensa, Deporte y Cultura de Masas. El Papel Del Periodismo Especializado En La Expansión Social Del Deporte En Cataluña Hasta La Guerra Civil (1890–1936)." *Historia y Comunicación Social* 17 (2012) *141–157,* 2012.

Rukeyser, Muriel. "We Came for Games." *Esquire*, October 1, 1974.

Rukeyser, Muriel, and Rowena Kennedy-Epstein. *Savage Coast: A Novel.* New York City: The Feminist Press, 2013.

Smith, A. *Red Barcelona: Social Protest and Labour Mobilization in the Twentieth Century.* Routledge, 2002.

Torres, Carles Santacana i, and Xavier Pujadas i Martí. *L'Altra Olimpíada, Barcelona'36: Esport, Societat i Política a Catalunya (1900–1936).* Llibres de l'Índex, 1990.

David C. Young. *A Brief History of the Olympic Games.* Wiley-Blackwell, 2004.

Zaagsma, Gerben. *Jewish Volunteers, the International Brigades and the Spanish Civil War.* Bloomsbury Publishing, 2017.

INDEX

© The Author(s) 2020

J. Stout, *The Popular Front and the Barcelona 1936 Popular Olympics*, Mega Event Planning,

https://doi.org/10.1007/978-981-13-8071-6

CPSIA information can be obtained
at www.ICGtesting.com
Printed in the USA
BVHW040343220120
570133BV00017B/426